THE STANDARD FOR PROGRAM MANAGEMENT

Fourth Edition

Library of Congress Cataloging-in-Publication Data has been applied for.

ISBN: 978-1-62825-196-8
    Published by: Project Management Institute, Inc.
                     18 Campus Boulevard
                     Newtown Square, Pennsylvania 19073-3299 USA
                     Phone: +610-356-4600
                     Fax: +610-356-4647
                     Email: customercare@pmi.org
                     Internet: www.PMI.org

To place a Trade Order or for pricing information, please contact Independent Publishers Group:
    Independent Publishers Group
    Order Department
    814 North Franklin Street
    Chicago, IL 60610 USA
    Phone: +1 800-888-4741
    Fax: +1 312- 337-5985
    Email: orders@ipgbook.com (For orders only)

10 9 8

NOTICE

The Project Management Institute, Inc. (PMI) standards and guideline publications, of which the document contained herein is one, are developed through a voluntary consensus standards development process. This process brings together volunteers and/or seeks out the views of persons who have an interest in the topic covered by this publication. While PMI administers the process and establishes rules to promote fairness in the development of consensus, it does not write the document and it does not independently test, evaluate, or verify the accuracy or completeness of any information or the soundness of any judgments contained in its standards and guideline publications.

PMI disclaims liability for any personal injury, property or other damages of any nature whatsoever, whether special, indirect, consequential or compensatory, directly or indirectly resulting from the publication, use of application, or reliance on this document. PMI disclaims and makes no guaranty or warranty, expressed or implied, as to the accuracy or completeness of any information published herein, and disclaims and makes no warranty that the information in this document will fulfill any of your particular purposes or needs. PMI does not undertake to guarantee the performance of any individual manufacturer or seller's products or services by virtue of this standard or guide.

In publishing and making this document available, PMI is not undertaking to render professional or other services for or on behalf of any person or entity, nor is PMI undertaking to perform any duty owed by any person or entity to someone else. Anyone using this document should rely on his or her own independent judgment or, as appropriate, seek the advice of a competent professional in determining the exercise of reasonable care in any given circumstances. Information and other standards on the topic covered by this publication may be available from other sources, which the user may wish to consult for additional views or information not covered by this publication.

PMI has no power, nor does it undertake to police or enforce compliance with the contents of this document. PMI does not certify, test, or inspect products, designs, or installations for safety or health purposes. Any certification or other statement of compliance with any health or safety-related information in this document shall not be attributable to PMI and is solely the responsibility of the certifier or maker of the statement.

TABLE OF CONTENTS

LIST OF TABLES AND FIGURES

1

INTRODUCTION

The Standard for Program Management – Fourth Edition provides guidance on the principles of program management. It provides generally accepted definitions of programs and program management and concepts important to their success—program management performance domains, the program life cycle, and important program management principles, practices, and activities. This edition of *The Standard for Program Management* expands and clarifies concepts presented in previous editions. It complements and aligns with the Project Management Institute's (PMI's) core foundational standards and guidance documents, including the latest edition of *A Guide to the Project Management Body of Knowledge (PMBOK® Guide)* [1],[1] *The Standard for Portfolio Management* [2], *Implementing Organizational Project Management: A Practice Guide* [3], and the *PMI Lexicon of Project Management Terms* [4].

This section defines and explains terms related to the standard's scope and provides an introduction to the content that follows. It includes the following major sections:

1.1 **Purpose of *The Standard for Program Management***

1.2 **What Is a Program?**

1.3 **What Is Program Management?**

1.4 **The Relationships among Portfolio, Program, and Project Management, and their Roles in Organizational Project Management (OPM)**

1.5 **The Relationships among Organizational Strategy, Program Management, and Operations Management**

1.6 **Business Value**

1.7 **Role of the Program Manager**

1.8 **Role of the Program Sponsor**

1.9 **Role of the Program Management Office**

---

[1] The numbers in brackets refer to the list of references at the end of this standard.

1.1 PURPOSE OF *THE STANDARD FOR PROGRAM MANAGEMENT*

The Standard for Program Management provides guidance on principles, practices, and activities of program management that are generally recognized to support good program management practices and that are applicable to most programs, most of the time.

◆ *Principles of program management* are tenets that are held to be true and important for the effective management of programs.

◆ *Generally recognized* means there is general consensus that the described principles, knowledge, and practices are valuable and useful.

◆ *Good practice* means there is general agreement that application of the principles, knowledge, and practices improves the management of programs and enhances the chances of program success, as measured by the extent and effectiveness of benefits delivery and realization. Good practice does not mean that all provisions of the standard are required to be applied to every program; an organization's leaders, its program managers, its program teams, and its program management office (when one is employed) are responsible for determining what is most appropriate for any given program, based on the unique or specific requirements of the program and its sponsoring organization.

The Standard for Program Management is also intended to provide a common understanding of the role of a program manager in general, and especially when interacting with:

◆ Portfolio managers whose portfolio(s) include the program or its components;

◆ Project managers whose projects are part of the program;

◆ Program sponsors and other members of the program steering committee. This committee may be referred to as a program or portfolio governance board;

◆ Program or project management office;

◆ Program team members working on the program or on other subsidiary programs;

◆ Program beneficiaries; and

◆ Other stakeholders or stakeholder groups (e.g., organizational executives, business partners, clients, suppliers, vendors, leaders or political groups) that may influence the program.

The Standard for Program Management is intended to be applied according to the Project Management Institute's *Code of Ethics and Professional Conduct* [5], which specifies obligations of responsibility, respect, fairness, and honesty that program managers should abide by in the conduct of their work. The *Code of Ethics and Professional Conduct* requires that practitioners demonstrate a commitment to ethical and professional conduct, and carries with it the obligation to comply with laws, regulations, and organizational and professional policies.

1.2 WHAT IS A PROGRAM?

A program is defined as related projects, subsidiary programs, and program activities managed in a coordinated manner to obtain benefits not available from managing them individually.

Managing projects, subsidiary programs, and program activities as a program enhances the delivery of benefits by ensuring that the strategies and work plans of program *components* are responsively adapted to component outcomes, or to changes in the direction or strategies of the sponsoring organization. Programs are conducted primarily to deliver benefits to the sponsor organizations or constituents of the sponsoring organization. Programs may deliver benefits, for example, by enhancing current capabilities, facilitating change, creating or maintaining assets, offering new products and services, or developing new opportunities to generate or preserve value. Such benefits are delivered to the sponsoring organization as outcomes that provide utility to the organization and the program's intended beneficiaries or stakeholders.

Programs deliver their intended benefits primarily through component projects and subsidiary programs that are pursued to produce outputs and outcomes. The components of a program are related through their pursuit of complementary goals that each contribute to the delivery of benefits.

Component projects or programs that do not advance common or complementary goals; or that do not jointly contribute to the delivery of common benefits; or that are related only by common sources of support, technology, or stakeholders are often better managed as portfolios rather than as programs (see *The Standard for Portfolio Management* [2]).

The following is a list of program elements and their definitions:

◆ **Components** are projects, subsidiary programs, or other related activities conducted to support a program.

◆ **Projects** are temporary endeavors undertaken to create a unique product, service, or result, as described fully in *A Guide to the Project Management Body of Knowledge (PMBOK® Guide)* [1]. Projects are used to generate the outputs or outcomes required by programs, within *defined constraints, such as budget, time, specifications, scope, and quality.*

◆ **Subsidiary programs**, sometimes referred to as subprograms, are programs sponsored and conducted to pursue a subset of goals important to the primary program. As an example, a program to develop a new electric car may sponsor other programs related to the development of new motor, battery, and charging station technologies. Each of these other programs would be managed as described in this standard and also monitored and managed as a component of the sponsoring program.

◆ **Other program-related activities** are work processes or activities that are being conducted to support a program, but that are not directly tied to the subsidiary programs or projects sponsored or conducted by a program. Examples of processes and activities sponsored by programs may include those related to training, planning, program-level control, reporting, accounting, and administration. Operational activities or maintenance functions that are directly related to a program's components may be considered as other program-related activities.

When used in the context of program management, the term activities should be read as program activities. Program activities are activities conducted to support a program, and not those activities performed during the course of a program's component projects.

The primary difference between projects and programs is based on the recognition within programs that the strategies for delivering benefits may need to be optimized adaptively as the outcomes of components are individually realized. The best mechanism for delivering a program's benefits may initially be ambiguous or uncertain. Outcomes delivered by a program's components contribute to the delivery of the program's intended benefits and, as necessary, to refinement of the strategy of the program and its components.

The primary value of managing an initiative as a program is based on the acknowledgement of the program manager's readiness to adapt strategies to optimize the delivery of benefits to an organization. As a consequence of a program's potential need to adapt to the outcomes and outputs of its components and its potential need to modify its strategy or plans, program components may be pursued in an iterative, nonsequential manner.

The program life cycle depicted in Figure 1-1 illustrates the nonsequential nature of a program's delivery phase. In a program, the iterative pursuit of components is expected to produce a stream of outputs and outcomes that contribute to organizational benefits. Program benefits may be realized incrementally throughout the duration of the program or may be realized at or after the end of the program. The program life cycle is discussed in greater detail in Section 7 of this standard.

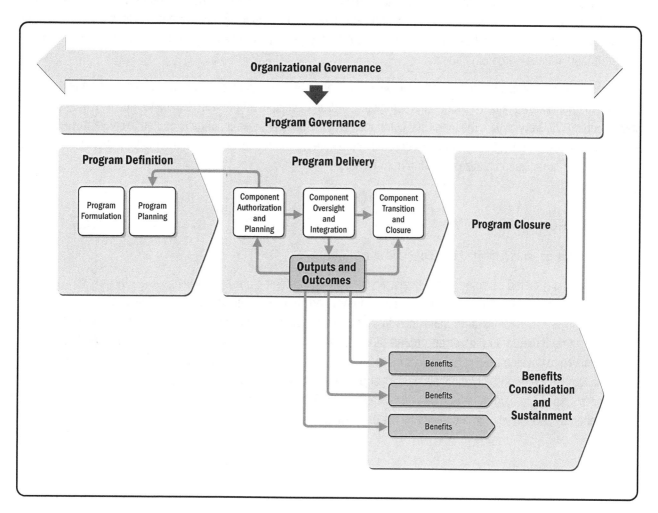

Figure 1-1. Program Life Cycle

One example of a program that delivers benefits incrementally is an organization-wide process improvement program. Such a program might be envisioned to pursue component projects to standardize and consolidate specific processes (e.g., financial control processes, inventory management processes, hiring processes, performance appraisal processes) and subsidiary programs to ensure that the benefits of consolidation are fully realized (e.g., to ensure adoption of the improved processes or to measure employee satisfaction and performance with the new processes). Each of these components may deliver incremental benefits as they are completed. The outcomes of components might trigger the initiation of new projects to further improve processes, satisfaction, and performance. However, the program would not be complete until all of the projects and subsidiary programs necessary for business improvement have delivered their intended program benefits.

Alternatively, programs may deliver intended benefits all at once—as a unified whole. In this case, the benefits of the program are not realized until the program is completed. A drug development program can be viewed as a program with unified benefits delivery, where the individual components of the program would not be expected to deliver benefits until the entire drug development program is successfully completed, the product is approved for sale, patients are treated with it, and the organization realizes benefits from its sale.

1.2.1 INITIATION OF PROGRAMS

Programs are generally initiated or recognized in two ways:

◆ Programs initiated to pursue new goals, objectives, or strategies are begun before the start of work on their component projects and programs. These programs are typically initiated to support new strategic goals and objectives; they enable an organization to pursue its vision and mission. Examples of such programs include programs initiated as part of an organization's strategic planning process (such as part of a portfolio-based decision to develop a new product or service, or to expand into a new market), to influence human behavior (such as to raise awareness of healthy behaviors or of terrorist threats, or to ensure compliance with new regulations), or to respond to a crisis (e.g., to provide disaster relief or to manage a public health issue). These programs are generally supported from the beginning by program management activities.

◆ Programs may also be formed when an organization recognizes that its ongoing projects, programs, and other work are related by their pursuit of common outcomes, capabilities, objectives, or benefits (e.g., a process improvement program supported by previously independent software development initiatives, or a neighborhood revitalization program supported by building public parks and traffic control projects, and a community outreach program). These programs are often formed when an organization determines that organizational benefits would be more effectively realized by managing ongoing initiatives as a single program. Such programs are supported by program management activities after some or all of their projects have been initiated.

Newly initiated or identified programs should all be managed according to the principles and life cycle management guidance described in the subsequent sections of this standard. It is incumbent on a program manager to ensure, for example, that activities important to program definition be completed for programs whose projects and other programs may have already begun.

1.2.2 THE RELATIONSHIPS AMONG PORTFOLIOS, PROGRAMS, AND PROJECTS

The relationship among portfolios, programs, and projects is as follows:

◆ A portfolio is a collection of projects, programs, subsidiary portfolios, and operations managed as a group to achieve strategic objectives.

◆ Programs consist of related projects, subsidiary programs, and program activities managed in a coordinated manner to obtain benefits not available from managing them individually. Programs are common elements of portfolios, conducted to deliver benefits important to an organization's strategic objectives.

◆ Projects, whether they are managed independently or as part of a program, are temporary endeavors that are undertaken to create unique products, services, or results.

Programs and projects, as significant elements of an organization's portfolio, are conducted to produce the outputs and outcomes required to support an organization's strategic objectives.

Figure 1-2 provides an example of how a portfolio of programs and projects may be organized to pursue an organization's strategy.

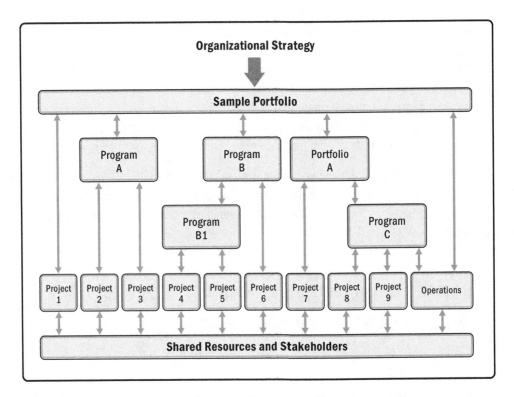

Figure 1-2. Example of Portfolios, Programs, and Projects and Organizational Strategy

1.3 WHAT IS PROGRAM MANAGEMENT?

Program management is defined as the application of knowledge, skills, and principles to a program to achieve the program objectives and to obtain benefits and control not available by managing program components individually. Program management involves the alignment of program components to ensure that program goals are achieved and program benefits are optimally delivered. Program management is performed by a program manager who is authorized by the organization to lead the team(s) responsible for achieving program goals and objectives.

The program manager ensures the effective alignment, integration, and control of a program's projects, subsidiary programs, and other program activities by actions taken in five interrelated and interdependent Program Management Performance Domains: Program Strategy Alignment, Program Benefits Management, Program Stakeholder Engagement, Program Governance, and Program Life Cycle Management. Program Management Performance Domains are complementary groupings of related areas of activity or function that uniquely characterize and differentiate the activities found in one performance domain from the others within the full scope of program management work. These performance domains are discussed in detail in subsequent sections of this standard. Through these Program Management Performance Domains, the program manager oversees and analyzes component interdependencies to determine the optimal approach for managing program components. Actions related to these interdependencies may include:

◆ Define how the outputs and outcomes of a program's components are expected to contribute to the program's delivery of its intended benefits and support the organization's strategy.

◆ Monitor benefits realization of program components to ensure they remain strategically aligned to the organization's goals.

◆ Ensure that the outputs and outcomes of a program's components are effectively communicated and considered so that a program can effectively optimize the pursuit of its intended benefits and provide value.

◆ Lead and coordinate program activities (for example, financing and procurement) across all program components, work, or phases.

◆ Communicate with and report to stakeholders to provide an integrated perspective on all activities being pursued within the program.

◆ Proactively assess and respond to risks spanning multiple components of the program.

◆ Align program efforts with the organizational strategy and the program's business case.

◆ Resolve scope, cost, schedule, resource, quality, and risk issues within a shared governance structure.

◆ Tailor program management activities, processes, and interfaces to effectively address cultural, socioeconomic, political, and environmental differences in programs.

Program managers apply program management principles to ensure that programs and their components are appropriately planned, controlled, and completed, and that program benefits are appropriately delivered and sustained.

1.4 THE RELATIONSHIPS AMONG PORTFOLIO, PROGRAM, AND PROJECT MANAGEMENT, AND THEIR ROLES IN ORGANIZATIONAL PROJECT MANAGEMENT (OPM)

To understand the relationships among portfolio, program, and project management, it is important to recognize the similarities and differences among these disciplines. It is also helpful to understand how they relate to organizational project management (OPM).

Portfolio, program, and project management all provide a structured means for organizations to align and effectively pursue organizational strategies. However, portfolio, program, and project management differ in their focus and in the way they contribute to the achievement of strategic goals.

◆ Portfolio management is the centralized management of one or more portfolios to achieve strategic objectives. Portfolio management focuses on the establishment and use of good practices when choosing programs or projects to sponsor, prioritizing their goals and work, and ensuring that they can be adequately resourced. Standards for the practice of portfolio management are described in *The Standard for Portfolio Management* [2].

◆ Program management is the application of knowledge, skills, and principles to a program to achieve the program objectives and to obtain benefits and control not available by managing program components individually. Program management focuses on the coordinated and effective delivery of benefits derived from the pursuit of a group of projects and other programs whose outcomes are related.

◆ Project management is the application of knowledge, skills, tools, and techniques to project activities to meet the project requirements. Project management focuses on the efficient delivery of the outputs and outcomes required by organizations within defined constraints of time, cost, and specifications. Standards for the practice of project management are described in *A Guide to the Project Management Body of Knowledge* [1].

OPM provides a framework in which portfolio, program, and project management practices are integrated to achieve strategic objectives. OPM supports the coordinated practice of portfolio, program, and project management by linking portfolio, program, and project management principles and practices. OPM is employed to produce improved performance, better results, and sustainable strategic benefits for organizations. OPM practices are described in *Implementing Organizational Project Management: A Practice Guide* [3].

Table 1-1 shows comparisons of the scope, focus, and management of portfolios, programs, and projects in the context of an organization. The distinctions between project and program management are discussed further in Section 2.5.

Table 1-1. Comparative Overview of Project, Program, and Portfolio Management

Organizational Project Management			
	Projects	**Programs**	**Portfolios**
Definition	A project is a temporary endeavor undertaken to create a unique product, service, or result.	A program is a group of related projects, subsidiary programs, and program activities that are managed in a coordinated manner to obtain benefits not available from managing them individually.	A portfolio is a collection of projects, programs, subsidiary portfolios, and operations managed as a group to achieve strategic objectives.
Scope	Projects have defined objectives. Scope is progressively elaborated throughout the project life cycle.	Programs have a scope that encompasses the scopes of its program components. Programs produce benefits to an organization by ensuring that the outputs and outcomes of program components are delivered in a coordinated and complementary manner.	Portfolios have an organizational scope that changes with the strategic objectives of the organization.
Change	Project managers expect change and implement processes to keep change managed and controlled.	Programs are managed in a manner that accepts and adapts to change as necessary to optimize the delivery of benefits as the program's components deliver outcomes and/or outputs.	Portfolio managers continuously monitor changes in the broader internal and external environments.
Planning	Project managers progressively elaborate high-level information into detailed plans throughout the project life cycle.	Programs are managed using high-level plans that track the interdependencies and progress of program components. Program plans are also used to guide planning at the component level.	Portfolio managers create and maintain necessary processes and communication relative to the aggregate portfolio.
Management	Project managers manage the project team to meet the project objectives.	Programs are managed by program managers who ensure that program benefits are delivered as expected, by coordinating the activities of a program's components.	Portfolio managers may manage or coordinate portfolio management staff, or program and project staff that may have reporting responsibilities into the aggregate portfolio.
Monitoring	Project managers monitor and control the work of producing the products, services, or results that the project was undertaken to produce.	Program managers monitor the progress of program components to ensure the overall goals, schedules, budget, and benefits of the program will be met.	Portfolio managers monitor strategic changes and aggregate resource allocation, performance results, and risk of the portfolio.
Success	Success is measured by product and project quality, timeliness, budget compliance, and degree of customer satisfaction.	A program's success is measured by the program's ability to deliver its intended benefits to an organization, and by the program's efficiency and effectiveness in delivering those benefits.	Success is measured in terms of the aggregate investment performance and benefit realization of the portfolio.

1.4.1 THE INTERACTIONS AMONG PORTFOLIO, PROGRAM, AND PROJECT MANAGEMENT

The distinctions among portfolio, program, and project management can be made clear through their interactions. Portfolio managers ensure that programs and projects are selected, prioritized, and staffed according to an organization's strategic plan for realizing desired organizational value. Program managers focus on delivering organizational benefits aligned with the organization's strategic plan through the coordinated management of projects, subsidiary programs, and other supportive work. Project managers focus on the generation of the specific outputs and outcomes required by an organization, as part of a project, a program, or a portfolio.

1.4.2 THE RELATIONSHIP BETWEEN PROGRAM MANAGEMENT AND PORTFOLIO MANAGEMENT

The relationship between program and portfolio management functions is collaborative. Program and portfolio managers work together to ensure that benefits desired or required by an organization are effectively and efficiently delivered. Organizational strategies and priorities established as part of portfolio management provide a basis for defining programs to be pursued, endorsing program strategies for delivering organizational benefits, and allocating the resources that programs require. Program strategies for delivering benefits define the specific means for pursuing organizational benefits and for defining the resources required from the organization. Together, the program and portfolio management functions support the organization by defining how an organization's strategic plans will be supported and delivered via appropriately prioritized and resourced programs.

1.4.3 THE RELATIONSHIP BETWEEN PROGRAM MANAGEMENT AND PROJECT MANAGEMENT

The relationship between program management and project management (as practiced by program and project managers) is also collaborative. Program and project managers work together to define viable strategies for pursuing program goals and thereby delivering program benefits. Program strategies and high-level program plans defined by program managers provide a basis for defining and authorizing projects that will be overseen by project managers. Projects managed by project managers deliver outputs and outcomes that provide a basis for reconfirming or adapting the strategic direction being pursued by the program and its components. Together, program and project managers support the organization by enabling the delivery of benefits that the organization desires or requires.

The interactions and relationships between program managers and project managers may change over the program life cycle. Projects may be initiated and completed at various times during the course of a program. During the initiation and planning stages of a project, it may be necessary for a program manager to work closely with a project manager providing oversight, direction, and guidance regarding the needs of the program. However, the relationship between program and project managers may be different during the work execution and closing phases of a project. During these phases, program managers typically focus more on coordinating interdependencies between the projects that contribute to their programs, while project managers focus on managing internal project activities. Program managers typically do not directly manage the individual project components on a day-to-day basis. As projects progress, the program manager's interactions with project managers focus more on identifying and controlling the interdependencies between projects; monitoring project performance; addressing escalated issues that impact component projects; and tracking the contributions of projects, subsidiary programs, and program work to the consolidated program benefits. At project closing, program and project managers again work closely to ensure that project outputs and outcomes are effectively transitioned to the program so that benefits delivered by a project are assimilated and sustained.

Program and project managers also collaborate in the management of issues and risk. The program manager monitors and addresses issues and risks that may impact program performance or benefits delivery and that cannot be addressed at the individual project or subsidiary program level. The project manager usually focuses on the management of issues and risks encountered within a given project. The project manager identifies issues, risks, and dependencies that (may) impact other program components to ensure that they are recognized by program managers.

Program managers also ensure that their programs recognize and embrace new opportunities that arise from the pursuit of program components.

The interactions between the program and project management functions tend to be iterative and cyclical:

- During a program's definition phase, information about the program's intended benefits, goals, and strategy flows from the program to its component projects; information about the strategies, objectives, needs, constraints, and timing of component projects flows back to the program.

- During the program's delivery phase, information about the progress, issues, risks, dependencies, outputs, and outcomes of component projects flows from the component project to the program and its other components. During this phase, the program management function communicates regularly with the project management function to ensure that the activities of all program components are appropriately coordinated and fully aligned with the program's intent to deliver organizational benefits.

- During the program's delivery and closure phases, as component projects are closed, information about project outputs and outcomes flows from the component project to the program to ensure that project benefits are fully realized and sustained.

The need for an iterative exchange of information and alignment of actions between program and project managers requires that the program and project management functions work closely together. A program manager may influence a project manager's approach for managing component projects based on the needs of the program and its other components.

1.5 THE RELATIONSHIPS AMONG ORGANIZATIONAL STRATEGY, PROGRAM MANAGEMENT, AND OPERATIONS MANAGEMENT

Organizations employ program management to pursue complex initiatives that support organizational strategy. In practice, when pursuing such initiatives, program managers also find that their programs impact lines of business that have operational responsibilities. Moreover, program managers often find that the benefits delivered by programs may influence an organization's approach to or scope of operational activities, and that program deliverables are transferred to organizational entities to ensure that their delivery of benefits is sustained. For these reasons, it is important that program managers establish collaborative, mutually supportive relationships with those responsible for managing operations within an organization. Together, program and operational managers are responsible for ensuring the balanced and successful execution of an organization's strategic objectives.

Organizations address the need for change by creating strategic business initiatives to produce results, or change the organization, its products, or its services. Portfolios of programs and projects are the vehicles for delivering these initiatives. For more information on the use of programs to produce change, see *Managing Change in Organizations: A Practice Guide* [6].

1.6 BUSINESS VALUE

Organizations employ program management to improve their abilities to deliver benefits. In noncommercial organizations, benefits may be delivered in the form of social or societal value (for example, improved health, safety, or security). In commercial organizations, it is common for organizational benefits to be delivered in the form of business value. Business value may be defined as the sum of all tangible and intangible elements of a business where, for example, tangible elements include monetary assets, facilities, fixtures, equity, tools, market share, and utility. Intangible elements may include goodwill, brand recognition, public benefit, trademarks, compliance, reputation, strategic alignment, and capabilities. Business value may also be created through the effective management of ongoing well-established operations. However, the effective use of portfolio, program, and project management enables organizations to employ reliable, established processes to generate new business value by enabling an organization to effectively pursue new business strategies consistent with its mission and vision for the future.

Portfolio management ensures that an organization's programs, projects, and operations are aligned with an organization's strategy. It allows organizations to define how they will pursue their strategic goals through programs and projects, and how those programs and projects will be supported by human, financial, technical, or material resources. In so doing, portfolio management optimizes the pursuit of business value.

Program management enables organizations to more effectively pursue their strategic goals through the coordinated pursuit of projects, subsidiary programs, and other program-related activities. Program management seeks to optimize the management of related component projects and programs to improve the generation of business value.

Project management enables organizations to more efficiently and effectively generate outputs and outcomes required for the pursuit of an organization's objectives by applying knowledge, processes, skills, tools, and techniques that enhance the delivery of outputs and outcomes by projects. Project management seeks to optimize the delivery of business value by improving the efficiency of organizations as they deliver new products, services, or results.

1.7 ROLE OF THE PROGRAM MANAGER

A program manager is the person authorized by the performing organization to lead the team or teams responsible for achieving program objectives. The program manager maintains responsibility for the leadership, conduct, and performance of a program, and for building a program team that is capable of achieving program objectives and delivering anticipated program benefits. The role of the program manager is different from that of the project manager. The differences between these roles are based on the fundamental differences between projects and programs and between project management and program management as described in Sections 1.2 through 1.4.

In programs, it is recognized that the best means of delivering benefits (via projects, subsidiary programs, and other work) may be uncertain. The outcomes or outputs generated by the components of programs may be unpredictable and uncontrollable. As a consequence, programs should be managed in a way that recognizes the potential need to adapt strategies and plans during the course of a program to optimize the delivery of benefits. A primary role of the program manager is to monitor the outputs and outcomes of a program's component activities and ensure that the program adapts appropriately to them. Program managers ensure that program components are adapted as required to meet the organization's strategic objectives.

The program manager is also responsible for managing or coordinating the management of complex issues that may arise as programs seek to deliver benefits. Such issues may result from uncertainties related to outcomes, operations, organizational strategies, resourcing, the external environment, organizational governance systems, or the expectations and motivations of program stakeholders.

The performance domains and supporting program activities described in Sections 3 through 7 discuss the principles, practices, and program management skills required for managing uncertainty, navigating complexity, and implementing change in the program environment, to optimize the delivery of program benefits. They describe a framework and the principles for engaging stakeholders and steering committees, and for managing the progression of a program's life cycle. Section 8 identifies supporting program activities recommended to facilitate the delivery of benefits.

In general, program managers are expected to:

◆ Work within the five Program Management Performance Domains.

◆ Interact with project and other program managers to provide support and guidance on individual initiatives conducted to support a program.

◆ Interact with portfolio managers to ensure that programs are provided with the appropriate resources and priority.

◆ Collaborate with governance bodies, sponsors and, (where applicable) the program management office to ensure the program's continued alignment with organizational strategy and ongoing organizational support.

◆ Interact with operational managers and stakeholders to ensure that programs receive appropriate operational support and that benefits delivered by the program can be effectively sustained.

◆ Ensure that the importance of each of a program's components is recognized and well understood.

◆ Ensure that the overall program structure and the applied program management processes enable the program and its component teams to successfully complete the work and deliver anticipated benefits.

◆ Integrate the program components' deliverables, outcomes, and benefits into the program's end product, services, or results, such that the program delivers its intended benefits.

◆ Provide effective and appropriate leadership to the program teams.

Program managers work to ensure that projects, other programs, and program activities are organized and executed in a consistent manner and fulfilled within established standards.

1.7.1 PROGRAM MANAGER COMPETENCES

To manage a program effectively, program managers need to encourage the efficient completion of project and other program activities as planned, while simultaneously enabling the adjustment of the strategy or plans of a program or its components whenever it will improve delivery of the program's intended benefits. Balancing these needs requires that program managers be competent in providing an integrated view of how the outputs and outcomes of program components will support the program's intended delivery of organizational benefits.

The expertise required of a program manager depends to a large degree on the proficiencies required to manage the complexity, ambiguity, uncertainty, and change associated with a program's outcomes or environment. The skills required may differ significantly among programs of different types, or even among programs of similar types facing dissimilar challenges. They may, for example, include technical skills specific to the program's targeted outcomes, business skills specific to the program's environment, or advanced project management skills critical to the management of complex operational challenges. The following skills and competences are commonly required by program managers:

◆ **Communication skills.** Communication skills that enable effective exchange of information with a wide variety of program stakeholders, including program team members, sponsors, customers, vendors, and senior management, whether individually or in groups or in committees.

◆ **Stakeholder engagement skills.** Stakeholder engagement skills to support the need to manage the complex issues that often arise as a consequence of stakeholder interactions. The program manager should recognize the dynamic aspects of managing individual and group expectations.

◆ **Change management skills.** Skills that enable effective engagement with individual stakeholders and governance and review committees, to gain the necessary agreements, alignment, and approvals when program strategies or plans need to be adapted. The program manager should provide an integrated view of the perspectives of stakeholders and committees whenever a program interacts with multiple committees as part of an organization's program review and approval process.

◆ **Leadership skills.** Leadership skills to guide program teams through the program life cycle. Program managers work with component managers and often with functional managers to gain support, resolve conflicts, and direct individual program team members by providing specific work instructions.

◆ **Analytical skills.** Skills that enable a program manager to assess whether the outputs and outcomes of program components will contribute as expected to the delivery of program benefits, or to assess the potential impact of external events on the program's strategy or plans.

◆ **Integration skills.** A program manager should possess the ability to describe and present a program's strategic vision and plan holistically. It is the program manager's responsibility to ensure the continuous alignment of the program component plans with the program's goals and pursuit of organizational benefits.

Skilled program managers who possess knowledge and experience in the program's area of focus generally will have an advantage over a program manager who lacks business-specific experience. Regardless of background, however, the successful program manager uses knowledge, experience, and leadership effectively to align the program's approach with the organization's strategy, improve the delivery of program benefits, enhance collaboration with stakeholders and program steering committees, and manage the program life cycle. In general, this requires the program manager to exhibit certain competences, including the abilities to:

◆ Manage details while taking a holistic, benefits-focused view of the program.

◆ Leverage a strong working knowledge of the principles, practices, processes, tools, and techniques of portfolio, program, and project management.

◆ Interact seamlessly and collaboratively with program steering committees and other executive stakeholders.

◆ Establish productive and collaborative relationships with team members and their organizational stakeholders.

◆ Leverage business knowledge, skills, and experience to provide perspectives that support the understanding and navigation of uncertainty, ambiguity, and complexity in the program environment.

◆ Facilitate understanding and agreement through the use of strong communication and negotiation skills.

Demonstrating these abilities within the context of a particular program or organization may present unique challenges. A program that is complex because of technical design issues may require a program manager with an engineering or technical background; a program that is complex because it involves many hundreds or thousands of interconnected activities may require a program manager with extensive background and experience in project management. Skilled program managers know their strengths and weaknesses and build a program management team that is complementary to their skill set.

Given the often complex and dynamic nature of programs, it is understandable that program managers may enter the field from the project management field or from a technical discipline closely related to their programs. Regardless of their path of entry to the field, program managers commonly seek specific development and training opportunities related to the key competences associated with the program manager role, such as PMI's Program Management Professional (PgMP)® credential program, or through post-graduate academic study.

For additional information regarding program management competences, refer to the *Project Manager Competency Development Framework* – Third Edition.

1.8 ROLE OF THE PROGRAM SPONSOR

A program sponsor is an individual or a group that provides resources and support for the program and is accountable for enabling success. A program steering committee may assume the role of a program sponsor. However, the program sponsor is usually an individual executive who is committed to ensuring that the program is appropriately supported and able to deliver its intended benefits. In this capacity, the sponsor may support and assist the program manager in stakeholder engagement. The program sponsor also provides valuable guidance and support to the program manager, ensuring that the program receives appropriate high-level attention and consideration, and that the program manager is informed of organizational changes that may affect the program. The governance and management-focused roles of the program sponsor are discussed in more detail in Sections 5.1 and 6.2.1, respectively.

1.9 ROLE OF THE PROGRAM MANAGEMENT OFFICE

A program management office is a management structure that standardizes the program-related governance processes and facilitates the sharing of resources, methodologies, tools, and techniques. A program management office often also supports training and other organizational change management activities. Program management offices may be established within an individual program to provide support specific to that program, or independent of an individual program to provide support to one or more of an organization's programs (for more detail, see Sections 5.1 and 6.2.3). When established as part of a program, a program management office is an important element of the program's infrastructure and an aid to the program manager. It may support the program manager with the management of multiple projects and program activities, for example, by:

◆ Defining standard program management processes and procedures that will be followed;

◆ Providing training to ensure that standards and practices are well understood;

◆ Supporting program communications;

◆ Supporting program level change management activities;

◆ Conducting program performance analyses;

◆ Supporting management of the program schedule and budget;

◆ Defining general quality standards for the program and its components;

◆ Supporting effective resource management;

◆ Providing support for reporting to leadership and program steering committees;

◆ Supporting document and knowledge transfer; and

◆ Providing centralized support for managing changes and tracking risks, issues, and decisions.

In addition, for large or complex programs, the program management office may provide additional management support for personnel and other resources, contracts and procurements, and legal or legislative issues.

Some programs continue for years and assume many aspects of normal operations that overlap with the larger organization's operational management. The program management office may take on some of these responsibilities. The specific governance and management-focused roles of the program management office are described further in Sections 6 and 8.

Some organizations elect not to have formally defined program management offices. In those instances, the managing function of the program management office is generally assumed by the assigned program manager.

2

PROGRAM MANAGEMENT PERFORMANCE DOMAINS

Program Management Performance Domains are complementary groupings of related areas of activity or function that uniquely characterize and differentiate the activities found in one performance domain from the others within the full scope of program management work.

This section includes:

2.1 Program Management Performance Domain Definitions

2.2 Program Management Performance Domain Interactions

2.3 Organizational Strategy, Portfolio Management, and Program Management Linkage

2.4 Portfolio and Program Distinctions

2.5 Program and Project Distinctions

Program managers actively carry out work within multiple Program Management Performance Domains during all program management phases.

The Program Management Performance Domains are shown in Figure 2-1: Program Strategy Alignment, Program Benefits Management, Program Stakeholder Engagement, Program Governance, and Program Life Cycle Management.

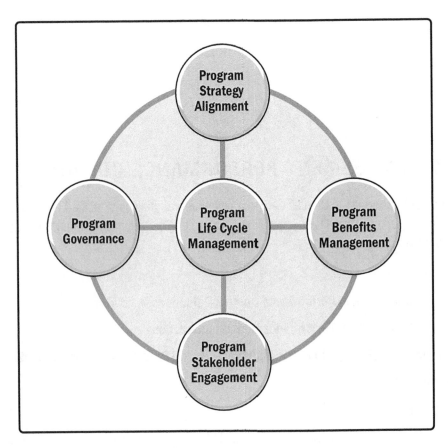

Figure 2-1. Program Management Performance Domains

2.1 PROGRAM MANAGEMENT PERFORMANCE DOMAIN DEFINITIONS

Organizations initiate programs to deliver benefits and accomplish agreed-upon objectives that often affect the entire organization. The organization implementing the program considers and balances the degree of needs, change, stakeholder expectations, requirements, resources, and timing conflicts across the components. Programs introduce change throughout their duration. This change may be reflected with the introduction of a new product, service, or organizational capability. Changes may be introduced to a variety of business processes (for example, the processes required to provide a new or improved service) through the actions, guidance, and leadership of the program manager working within the five Program Management Performance Domains. Together, these performance domains are critical to the success of the program. Definitions of the Program Management Performance Domains are as follows:

◆ **Program Strategy Alignment**—Performance domain that identifies program outputs and outcomes to provide benefits aligned with the organization's goals and objectives.

◆ **Program Benefits Management**—Performance domain that defines, creates, maximizes, and delivers the benefits provided by the program.

◆ **Program Stakeholder Engagement**—Performance domain that identifies and analyzes stakeholder needs and manages expectations and communications to foster stakeholder support.

◆ **Program Governance**—Performance domain that enables and performs program decision making, establishes practices to support the program, and maintains program oversight.

◆ **Program Life Cycle Management**—Performance domain that manages program activities required to facilitate effective program definition, program delivery, and program closure.

These domains run concurrently throughout the duration of the program. It is within these domains that the program manager and the program team perform their activities. The nature and the complexity of the program being implemented determine the degree of activity required within a particular domain at any particular point in time. Every program requires some activity in each of these performance domains during the entire course of the program. Work within these domains is iterative in nature and is repeated frequently. Each domain is described in detail in its respective section within this standard.

2.2 PROGRAM MANAGEMENT PERFORMANCE DOMAIN INTERACTIONS

As introduced previously and depicted in Figure 2-1, all five Program Management Performance Domains interact with each other throughout the course of the program. How much interaction there will be and when it should occur will depend upon the program and its components. The amount of interaction for any given program is as varied as the number of programs that exist. When organizations pursue similar programs, the interactions among the performance domains are similar and often repetitive. All five domains interact with each other with varying degrees of intensity. These domains are the areas in which program managers will spend their time while implementing the program. The five domains reflect the higher-level business functions that are essential aspects of the program manager's role regardless of the size of the organization, industry or business focus, and/or geographic location.

2.3 ORGANIZATIONAL STRATEGY, PORTFOLIO MANAGEMENT, AND PROGRAM MANAGEMENT LINKAGE

Programs typically find their starting point during an organization's strategic planning effort, where the full spectrum of the organization's investments are evaluated, prioritized, and aligned with the organization's operational strategy. As the business climate or organizational strategy changes, organizations continue to evaluate work through portfolio reviews, by reinforcing components of the portfolio that are in alignment and are achieving intended benefits and organizational objectives, and closing initiatives that are not aligned with organizational objectives. New initiatives that have the potential for contributing to the overall forward progress and success of the organization are proposed and analyzed during the portfolio review process and create the starting point for new projects, portfolio components, and programs.

During an organization's portfolio review process, programs are evaluated to ensure that they continue to support an organization's strategy and objectives and that they are performing as expected. Programs are typically reviewed to ensure the program's business case, charter, and benefits management plan reflect the current and most suitable profile of the intended outcomes. A concept may be approved for a limited time with limited funding to develop a business case for further evaluation. The business case is then reviewed during the portfolio review process. This occurs during the program formulation subphase of the program life cycle. When the actual program is approved, funding is formally approved and allocated, and a program manager is assigned to the initiative. During the program delivery phase, program components are initiated, planned, executed, transitioned, and closed, while benefits are delivered, transitioned, and sustained. During this phase, individual projects and subsidiary programs within the program may begin and end as the program continues during the delivery of benefits. The program is closed when the desired benefits are achieved or when reasons for closure arise. Programs may close when the benefits and objectives to be achieved by the program are no longer in alignment with the organization's strategy or when measurements against the program's key performance indicators reveal that the business case for the program is no longer viable.

2.4 PORTFOLIO AND PROGRAM DISTINCTIONS

While portfolios and programs are both collections of projects, activities, and non-project work, there are aspects that clearly differentiate them and help clarify the differences between the two. As defined in Section 1, a program is a group of related projects, other programs, and program activities managed in a coordinated way to obtain benefits not available from managing them individually. To clarify the difference between these important organizational constructs, two aspects stand out: relatedness and time.

◆ **Relatedness.** A primary consideration that differentiates programs and portfolios is the concept introduced and implied by the word "related" in the definition of program. In a program, the work included is interdependent such that achieving the full intended benefits is dependent on the delivery of all components in the scope of the program. In a portfolio, the work included is related in any way the portfolio owner chooses. Typical portfolio groupings of work include efforts staffed from the same resource pool, work delivered to the same client, or work conducted in the same accounting period. Other groupings are also valid, for example, work performed within the same geographical area or strategic business unit. Work included in the portfolio may span a variety of diverse initiatives, and these initiatives can be independent. Though the initiatives may be entirely independent and not related to one another in any way, the organization may group and manage them together for ease of oversight and control.

◆ **Time.** Another attribute that differentiates portfolios from programs is the element of time. Programs, like projects, are temporary and include the concept of time as an aspect of the work. Though they may span multiple years or decades, programs are characterized by the existence of a clearly defined beginning, a future endpoint, and a set of outcomes and planned benefits that are to be achieved during the conduct of the program. Portfolios, on the other hand, while being reviewed on a regular basis for decision-making purposes, are not expected to be constrained to end on a specific date. The various initiatives and work elements defined within portfolios mostly do not directly relate to one another and do not rely on each other to achieve benefits. In portfolios, the organization's strategic plan and business cycle dictate the start or end of specific investments, and these investments may serve widely divergent objectives. Additionally, work and investments within the portfolio may continue for years or decades, or may be altered or terminated by the organization as the business environment changes. Finally, portfolios contain proposals for various initiatives, including programs and projects that should be evaluated and aligned with the organization's strategic objectives before they are approved. A proposal may exist in the organization's portfolio for an indeterminate length of time.

To summarize, programs differ from portfolios in two important ways. Programs include work (projects, subsidiary programs, and program activities) that are related in some way and collectively contribute to the achievement of the program's outcomes and intended benefits. Programs also include the concept of time and incorporate schedules through which specific milestone achievements are measured. Portfolios do not require the work within the portfolio to be related and are managed in an ongoing fashion as initiatives (programs and projects) are introduced to the portfolio and are subsequently completed. Portfolios provide a means for organizations to effectively manage a collection of investments and work that is important to the achievement of the organization's strategic objectives.

2.5 PROGRAM AND PROJECT DISTINCTIONS

As described in Section 1, program management provides organizations with an effective framework for managing interrelated groupings of work (i.e., projects, subsidiary programs, and program activities) designed to produce benefits not achievable by managing the work as individual initiatives. Programs are often large, complex, lengthy, and accept uncertainty in their definition. This section further discusses three characteristics that distinguish programs from projects. These fundamental differences are found in the way programs and projects are managed in response to uncertainty, change, and complexity.

2.5.1 UNCERTAINTY

Uncertainty is an inevitable challenge of managing programs. Uncertainty is especially high in the beginning of a program as the outcomes are not clear. Programs and projects both exist in organizational environments in which the output, benefits, or outcome of the work may be somewhat unpredictable or uncertain. Changes external to the organizational environment also create uncertainty, which increases the uncertainty of managing programs. Within the context of the organization, however, individual projects may be considered to be more certain than programs.

The expected outputs of projects are generally more certain than those of programs at the time of their inception. This can be attributed to the project's fixed constraints. As a project proceeds, its ability to deliver those outputs on time, on budget, and according to specification becomes more certain as a result of the progressive elaboration that removes uncertainty during the course of the project. By contrast, a program may not have its entire scope, budget, or timeline determined upon preparation. This in turn can be addressed by the program's ability to deal with uncertainty because programs can change the direction of projects, cancel projects, or start new projects to adapt to changing circumstances. This ability creates uncertainty about the program's direction and outcome. During the program, scope and content are continually elaborated, clarified, and adjusted to ensure the program's outcomes remain in alignment with the intended benefits. This results in an initial program environment that is recognized to be uncertain, and implies the need for a management style that embraces uncertainty in order to address it more effectively. The program may include individual components that meet or fulfill all their success criteria: providing outputs, products, or services precisely as planned. However, in the context of the program's outcomes and intended benefits, these individual components may not contribute at all to the outcomes that were anticipated. This creates additional uncertainty about the outcomes the program may achieve.

With the focus on benefits realization and the multiple components that work together to produce the intended outcomes, the complexity and duration of the program demand that the program manager take a broad, collective view of all the program's components to thoroughly understand and successfully manage the progress and contributions of the component parts. This distinguishes and differentiates the program management and project management approaches, and explains the need for both within a program.

2.5.2 MANAGING CHANGE

Program managers need to consider two different categories of change. These will be referred to as internal change and external change. Internal change refers to changes within the program. External change refers to the need to adapt the organization in order for it to be able to exploit the benefits created by the program.

Issues related to change should be addressed differently within programs and projects. Projects deal with change in terms of scope, time, cost, and quality. As with uncertainty, programs should be better equipped to deal with change because they have the ability to change the direction of a component, cancel a component, or start a new component. In both programs and projects, there should be a rationale that justifies that the advantages originating from a proposed change will outweigh potential drawbacks. Change within a project affects the defined deliverables at the tactical level, whereas change within a program affects the delivery of the intended benefits at the strategic level. Managing change within a program requires strategic insight and understanding of the program's objectives and intended benefits. Change to any component within a program may have a direct impact on the delivery of the other related components, which necessitates a change in those specific components. Change of a project is generally local to the project and related to the tactical level.

In programs, change management is a key activity, enabling stakeholders to carefully analyze the need for proposed change, the impact of change, and the approach or process for implementing and communicating change. The change management plan, which is part of the program management plan and developed during program preparation, establishes the change management authorities.

◆ **Program change.** Program managers approach change at the program level in a fundamentally different way. Program managers depend on a predetermined, consistent level of performance from the components of the program. For components that are projects, program managers rightfully expect the projects to be delivered on time, on budget, within scope, and with an acceptable level of quality. For other programs and program activities, the program manager should require that each be performed in a manner that will contribute positively to the program's outcome and anticipated benefits or reduce the negative outcome. For program components, just as in projects, change management is employed to understand and control the variability of each component's schedule, cost, and output. In addition, program managers can create new components or cancel existing components. This change is made to ensure the optimal delivery of benefits.

◆ **Project change.** In projects, change management is employed to help the project manager, team, and stakeholders monitor and control the amount of variance from the planned cost and schedule while protecting the approved attributes and characteristics of the planned output. If a change is required that impacts the scope (including deliverables), cost, schedule, quality, or expected results, then a project change request is developed to modify the scope, schedule, cost, or intended output (deliverable) of the project. If accepted, the change is incorporated into the structure of the project, and the cost, schedule, and attributes are adjusted to accommodate all aspects of the change. The project is then replanned and the updated cost, schedule, and deliverable specifications become the new baseline for the project. Once the project change request is completed and accepted, change management is employed to ensure the project remains aligned with the new baseline(s). Projects also use change management to manage the impact of variance caused by known risks that were triggered (expected events) and unknown risks that were triggered (unexpected events) on its path to a project's completion.

Given the consistent delivery of the program's components, the program manager addresses the uncertainty of the overall program's outcomes and anticipates that it is possible that some of the program's components will be successfully delivered, but will produce entirely unexpected results—results that may or may not contribute positively to the intended benefits of the program. In order to address the program's inherent uncertainty, the program manager may group individual components into other programs to manage them more effectively. In addition, the program manager may redirect, replan, or stop individual efforts entirely, knowing they will not help achieve the desired program benefits if left unattended in the context of the evolving environment. When this occurs, the program manager employs change management at the program level to redirect and modify the roadmap of the program to ensure it aligns with the expected benefits to be delivered, the new strategy, the social, regulatory or economic state, or the perceptions of the program's beneficiaries.

Programs use change management in a forward-looking, proactive manner to adapt to the evolving environment. This is an iterative process repeated frequently during the performance of a program to ensure the program delivers the benefits planned at the start of the program.

To summarize, projects employ change and change management to constrain or control the impact of variability on their baselines, while programs proactively use change management to keep the program components and intended benefits aligned with changes in organizational strategy and changes in the environment in which they are performed.

2.5.3 COMPLEXITY

Both programs and projects are associated with complexity. The sources of complexity within programs and projects can be grouped into human behavior, system behavior, and ambiguity (See *Navigating Complexity: A Practice Guide*). The factors that result in program and project complexity originate from these two groupings.

- ◆ **Program complexity.** The complexity of a program may be the result from a combination of factors.

  - ■ *Governance complexity.* Governance complexity results from the sponsor support for the program as well as the support of the related components' sponsors, management structures, number of organizations involved and the decision-making processes within the program.

  - ■ *Stakeholder complexity.* Stakeholder complexity arises from the differences in the needs and influence of stakeholders, which may be a burden to the program or in conflict with the benefits of the program. Stakeholder complexity also focuses on the program team itself and the diversity within the program team. Stakeholder complexity is also associated with the number of stakeholders interested in the program.

  - ■ *Definition complexity.* Programs bring about change, and definition complexity focuses on the agreement of the future state by stakeholders. Other aspects that the program manager should be cognizant of include benefits management and the potential competing interests of stakeholders.

  - ■ *Benefits delivery complexity.* Benefits delivery complexity focuses on benefits management, as discussed in Section 4.

  - ■ *Interdependency complexity.* Program managers need to deal with interdependency complexity. A program focuses on the interdependencies among components and not necessarily on issues within individual projects. Programs strengthen and enforce interdependencies among components to ensure that the overall outcome of the program delivers the intended benefits. Interdependencies among components and other business entities should be clearly defined. Program managers focus on interdependencies that occur within the program and its related projects. Interdependencies can also occur outside the program when there are dependencies on other projects or programs as well as dependencies external to the organization. Interdependencies are directly related to the complexity of the program.

- *Resource complexity.* The availability of resources at the required level of capability and capacity, adequate funding, and suitable supplies and materials add to the complexity of the program, and these resource concerns need to be addressed within the program.

- *Scope complexity.* Scope complexity arises from the difficulty to clearly define the deliverables and benefits of a program and its components. Managing the delivery of the associated benefits beyond the lifespan of the program's components contributes to scope complexity.

- *Change complexity.* Change complexity arises from the different levels of impact the change potentially can cause in an organization. Change complexity is low when a program changes the basic operational processes model in one or two departments, but can be extremely complex when a program transforms an organization from a functional to a projectized organization.

- *Risk complexity.* Risk complexity arises from the high level of uncertainty due to the extended program life cycle and the uncertainty of the components' outcome and their interdependencies.

◆ **Project complexity.** A project can be complex because of the uniqueness it presents as well as the kind of thinking, action, and knowledge needed in order to solve a problem or complete a task. This uniqueness creates uncertainty with regard to time and costing estimates, as well as the specifications needed to deliver the desired project output and outcomes. Project complexity can be characterized as organizational or dynamic complexity.

  - *Organizational complexity.* Organizational complexity focuses on the depth of the organizational structure as well as the number of organizational units. It also addresses the number and types of elements and their relationships in the organization.

  - *Dynamic complexity.* Dynamic complexity focuses on the project's behavior and how it changes over time.

3

—

PROGRAM STRATEGY ALIGNMENT

Program Strategy Alignment is the performance domain that identifies program outputs and outcomes to provide benefits aligned with the organization's strategic goals and objectives.

This section includes:

3.1 Program Business Case

3.2 Program Charter

3.3 Program Roadmap

3.4 Environmental Assessments

3.5 Program Risk Management Strategy

Programs are designed to align with the organizational strategy and to facilitate the realization of organizational benefits. To accomplish this, program managers need to have a thorough understanding of how the program will fulfill the portfolio and organization's strategy, goals and objectives, and the skills needed to align the program with the long-term goals of the organization.

When an organization develops its strategy, there is typically an initial evaluation and selection process that may be formal or informal to help the organization determine which initiatives to approve, deny, or defer as part of the portfolio management practice of the organization.

The more mature an organization is in terms of program and project management, the more likely it will have a formalized process for program selection such as a portfolio review board or a program steering committee. Either decision-making body may issue a program charter that defines the strategic objectives and benefits a particular program is expected to deliver. The program charter is a document issued by a sponsor that authorizes the program management team to use organizational resources to execute the program and links the program to the organization's strategic objectives. It defines the scope and purpose of a proposed program presented to governance to obtain approval, funding, and authorization. This program charter confirms the commitment of organizational resources to determine if a program is the most appropriate approach for achieving these objectives and triggers the program definition phase.

While project managers lead and direct the work on their projects, it is the program manager's responsibility to ensure alignment of individual project management plans with the program's goals and intended benefits to support the achievement of the organization's strategic goals and objectives.

Figure 3-1 depicts the components of Program Strategy Alignment.

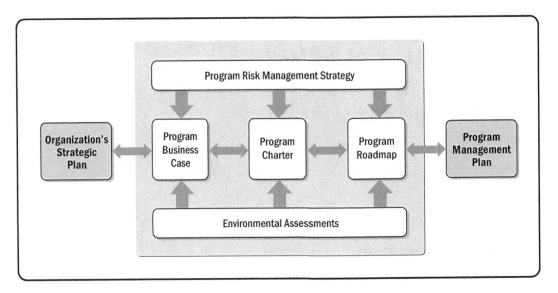

Figure 3-1. Elements of Program Strategy Alignment

Program Strategy Alignment is initiated with the development of a program business case. A program business case is a documented economic feasibility study used to establish validity of the benefits to be delivered by a program; it justifies the need for a program by defining how a program's expected outcomes would support the organization's strategic goals and objectives. As the documented economic feasibility study is used to establish validity of the benefits to be delivered by a program, the business case is then further used as an input to the program charter and subsequently the program roadmap. These three documents are established as part of program formulation activities (see Section 7.1.2.1).

During the execution of the program formulation subphase, the program strategy alignment process is initiated and runs until the end of the program life cycle. During this time, the management processes to identify and quantify environmental factors, outcomes, and benefits and to identify and manage program risks are executed and controlled within the program governance framework. When misalignment is identified, the program management plan or organization's strategic goals and objectives should be revised to ensure alignment. This may occur in research, where the results of a program determine that a given line of research is not likely to succeed, and the organization then changes its strategy—sometimes without canceling or discontinuing the program—to better leverage the results of the program.

3.1 PROGRAM BUSINESS CASE

Organizations build strategy to define how their vision will be achieved. The completion of the strategic planning cycle results in the creation or update of the organization's strategic goals and objectives which is documented in the organization's strategic plan. The organization's vision and mission are used as input to the strategic planning cycle and are reflected throughout the strategic plan. The organization's strategic plan is subdivided into a set of organizational initiatives that are influenced in part by market dynamics, customer and partner requests, shareholders, government regulations, organization's strengths and weaknesses, risk exposure, and competitor plans and actions. These initiatives may be grouped into portfolios to be executed during a predetermined period.

Programs are formally evaluated, selected, and authorized based on their alignment and support to achieve the organization's strategic plan, usually as part of the organization's governance practices. To facilitate alignment and goal setting, the organization's strategic plan is further delineated as a set of goals and objectives that may have measurable elements such as products, deliverables, benefits, cost, and timing, among others. The goal of linking the program to the organization's strategic plan is to plan and manage a program that will help the organization achieve its strategic goals and objectives and to balance its use of resources while maximizing value. This is achieved through the business case. During program definition, the program manager collaborates with key sponsors and stakeholders to develop the program's business case. This business case is developed to assess the program's investment against the intended benefits. The business case can be basic and high-level or detailed and comprehensive. It usually describes key parameters that can be used to assess the objectives and constraints for the intended program.

The business case may include details about the program outcomes, approved concept, issues, high-level risk and opportunity assessment, key assumptions, business and operational impact, cost benefit analysis, alternative solutions, financial analysis, intrinsic and extrinsic benefits, market demands or barriers, potential profits, social needs, environmental influences, legal implications, time to market, constraints, and the extent to which the program aligns with the organization's strategic plan. The business case describes the intent and authority behind the drivers of the program and underlying philosophy of the business need. The business case also serves as a formal declaration of the value that the program is expected to deliver and a justification for the resources that will be expended to deliver it.

The business case is required as one of the document deliverables before the program can be formally chartered and may be considered as the primary justification document for an investment decision. Also, the business case describes success criteria that is maintained throughout the program. The variance between the achieved and the planned outcomes is calculated to measure the success of the program.

3.2 PROGRAM CHARTER

Following the approval of the business case, the program steering committee (see Section 5.1) authorizes the program by means of the program charter. Derived from the business case, the program charter is a document that assigns and authorizes a program manager and defines the scope and purpose of a proposed program presented to governance to obtain approval, funding, and authorization.

Key elements of a program charter consist of the program scope, assumptions, constraints, high-level risks, high-level benefits, goals and objectives, success factors, timing, key stakeholders, and other provisions that tie the program to the business case, thereby enabling program strategy alignment. (See Section 7.1.2.1 for more information on the contents of a program charter.)

The program charter formally expresses the organization's vision, mission, and benefits expected to be produced by the program; it also defines program-specific goals and objectives in alignment with the organization's strategic plan in support of the business case. The program charter also provides the program manager with the authority for leading other subsidiary programs, projects, and related activities to be initiated, in addition to the framework by which these program components will be managed and monitored during the course of the program. The program charter is one of the document deliverables that will be used to measure program success. It should include the metrics for success, a method for measurement, and a clear definition of success.

3.3 PROGRAM ROADMAP

While planning the program, the program manager analyzes available information about the organization's strategic goals and objectives, internal and external influences, program drivers, and the benefits that stakeholders expect the program to realize. The program is defined in terms of expected outcomes, required resources, and strategy for delivering the needed changes to implement new capabilities across the organization.

The program roadmap (see Figure 3-2) is a chronological representation of a program's intended direction, graphically depicting dependencies between major milestones and decision points, which reflects the linkage between the business strategy and the program work.

While elements of a program roadmap are similar to a project schedule, the roadmap instead outlines major program events for the purposes of planning and the development of more detailed schedules. The program roadmap also reflects the pace at which benefits are realized and serves as a basis for transition and integration of new capabilities.

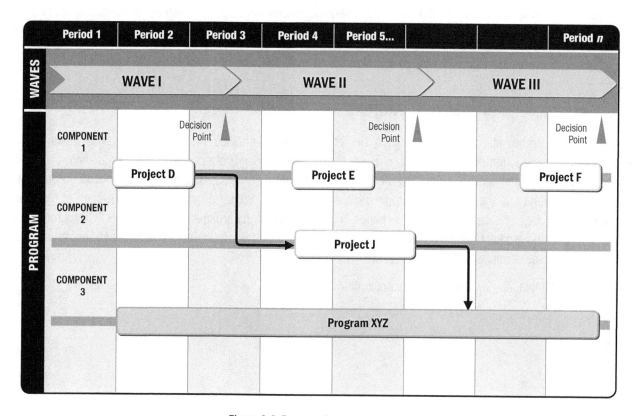

Figure 3-2. Program Roadmap Example

The program roadmap can be a valuable tool for managing the organization of a program and for assessing a program's progress toward achieving its expected benefits. To better enable effective governance of the program, the program roadmap can be used to show how benefits are delivered within major stages or milestones; however, it may include the component details, their durations, and contributions to benefits. In a large construction program, for example, the roadmap may present stages of construction toward the final benefits of the construction. In a system development and production program, the program roadmap may depict how benefits such as system capabilities will be delivered through incremental releases or a series of models. A roadmap is an effective way to communicate the overarching plan and benefits to stakeholders to build and maintain advocacy.

3.4 ENVIRONMENTAL ASSESSMENTS

There are often internal or external influences to the program that have a significant impact on a program's success. Influences from outside the program may be internal to the larger organization, or may come from sources external to the organization. Program managers should identify these influences and take them into account when managing the program in order to ensure ongoing stakeholder alignment, the program's continued alignment with the organization's strategic goals and objectives, and overall program success.

3.4.1 ENTERPRISE ENVIRONMENTAL FACTORS

Enterprise environmental factors external to the program may influence the selection, design, funding, and management of a program. Enterprise environmental factors refer to conditions, not under the immediate control of the team, that influence, constrain, or direct the program. A program should be selected and prioritized according to how well it supports the organization's strategic goals and objectives. Strategic goals change, however, in response to environmental factors. When this occurs, a change in the direction of the organization may cause the program to be misaligned with the organization's revised strategic plan. In this case, the program may be changed, put on hold, or canceled regardless of how well it was performing.

Environmental factors may include but are not limited to:

◆ Business environment;

◆ Market;

◆ Funding;

◆ Resources;

◆ Industry;

◆ Health, safety, and environment;

◆ Economy;

◆ Cultural diversity;

◆ Geographic diversity;

◆ Regulatory;

◆ Legislative;

◆ Growth;

◆ Supply base;

◆ Technology;

◆ Political influence;

- ◆ Audit;

- ◆ New business processes, standards, and practices; and

- ◆ Discoveries and inventions.

Consideration of these factors and their associated uncertainty or change helps the ongoing assessment and evolution of an organization and the alignment of its programs with its goals. The ongoing management of a program should include continual monitoring of the environmental factors to ensure the program remains aligned with the organization's strategic objectives.

3.4.2 ENVIRONMENTAL ANALYSIS

The following sections outline various forms of analysis that may be used to assess the validity of a program's business case and program management plan. Consideration of the results from one or more environmental analyses enables the program manager to highlight factors that have potential for impacting the program and informs risk management. Sections 3.4.2.1 through 3.4.2.5 are provided as representative samples of environmental analyses that may be performed or commissioned by the program manager. The activities included are not intended to be comprehensive or all-inclusive.

3.4.2.1 COMPARATIVE ADVANTAGE ANALYSIS

When conducting environmental analysis for a strategic initiative and/or business case, it is important to consider that competing efforts may reside within or external to the organization. A typical business case includes analysis and comparison against real or hypothetical alternative scenarios. Where appropriate, comparative advantage analysis may also include what-if analyses to illustrate how the program's objectives and intended benefits could be achieved by other means.

3.4.2.2 FEASIBILITY STUDIES

Using the business case, organizational goals, and other existing initiatives as a base, this process assesses the feasibility of the program within the organization's financial, sourcing, complexity, and constraint profile. This analysis contributes to the body of information that decision makers require to approve or deny the program proposal.

3.4.2.3 SWOT ANALYSIS

An analysis of the strengths, weaknesses, opportunities, and threats (SWOT) faced by a program provides information for optimizing the program charter and program management plan. The SWOT analysis, in particular the analysis of weaknesses and threats, may be a valuable input to the development of the program risk management strategy. SWOT analysis may also form part of the feasibility study as well as the business case.

3.4.2.4 ASSUMPTIONS ANALYSIS

Assumptions are factors that, for planning purposes, are considered true, real, or certain. Identified initially during business case development, assumptions affect all aspects of the program and are part of the progressive elaboration of the program. Program managers regularly identify and document assumptions as part of their planning process. In addition, assumptions should be validated during the course of the program to ensure that the assumptions have not been invalidated by events or other program activities.

3.4.2.5 HISTORICAL INFORMATION ANALYSIS

Previously completed programs and completed phases of active programs may be a source of lessons learned and best practices for new programs (refer to Section 8.2.4.1.). Historical information includes artifacts, metrics, risks, and estimations from previous programs, projects, and ongoing operations that may be relevant to the current program. Historical information describing the successes, failures, and lessons learned is particularly important during program definition.

3.5 PROGRAM RISK MANAGEMENT STRATEGY

Successful delivery of the program roadmap, aligned with organizational strategy, and with consideration to the environmental factors found in the environmental assessments, depends on a well-defined program risk strategy.

While Section 8 details the program risk management activities, this section addresses the specific program risk management strategy that drives the program risk management activities (actively identifying, monitoring, analyzing, accepting, mitigating, avoiding, or retiring program risk) to ensure the program is aligned with organizational strategy.

3.5.1 RISK MANAGEMENT FOR STRATEGY ALIGNMENT

Strategy alignment comprises the alignment of the program roadmap and its supported objectives to organizational strategy. This involves having a risk management strategy that ensures effective management of any risk that can cause the program to be out of alignment with organizational strategy. Such a risk management strategy includes defining program risk thresholds, performing the initial program risk assessment, and developing a high-level program risk response strategy, as well as determining how risks will be communicated to strategic levels of the organization. Strategy alignment requires program risk thresholds to take into account the organization's strategy including its risk appetite, which is an assessment of the organization's willingness to accept and deal with risks (see Section 8.1.1.7).

3.5.2 PROGRAM RISK THRESHOLDS

Risk threshold is the measure of the degree of acceptable variation around a program objective that reflects the risk appetite of the organization and program stakeholders.

As previously mentioned, a key element of program risk strategy is the establishment and monitoring of program risk thresholds. Examples of program risk thresholds include:

◆ Minimum level of risk exposure for a risk to be included in the risk register,

◆ Qualitative (high, medium, low, etc.) or quantitative (numerical) definitions of risk rating, and

◆ Maximum level of risk exposure that can be managed within the program (beyond which an escalation is triggered).

Establishing program risk thresholds is an integral step in linking program risk management to strategy alignment and therefore should be done as part of early planning. Based on the risk appetite of the organization, program governance, working in collaboration with corporate governance and the program management team may also be responsible for ensuring that program risk thresholds are established and observed in the program (see Section 6.1.6).

3.5.3 INITIAL PROGRAM RISK ASSESSMENT

While program risk management is conducted throughout the life of the program, the initial program risk assessment, prepared during program definition, offers a unique opportunity to identify risks to organizational strategy alignment. It enables risk to be considered when developing the program roadmap and when examining environmental factors. As such, it is critical that the initial program risk assessment identifies any risk to strategy alignment, which includes but is not limited to any uncertain events or conditions that, if they occur, could lead to:

◆ Program objectives not supportive of organizational objectives,

◆ Program roadmap not aligned with organizational roadmap,

◆ Program roadmap not supportive of portfolio roadmaps,

◆ Program objective not supportive of portfolio objectives, and

◆ Program resource requirements out of sync with organizational capacity and capability.

Once the initial program risk assessment is performed, a risk response strategy is developed to complete the program risk management strategy.

3.5.4 PROGRAM RISK RESPONSE STRATEGY

Program risk response strategy combines the elements of the risk thresholds and the initial risk assessment into a plan for how program risks will be managed effectively and consistently throughout the life of the program. For each identified risk, the risk thresholds can be used to identify the specific response strategy based on a number of rating criteria. As an example, for an organization that views 5 % schedule variance as acceptable:

◆ Risk threshold—5% schedule delay,

◆ Risk rating—no significant risk, and

◆ Response strategy—accept.

A robust program risk management strategy comprises a specific risk response strategy for each of the risk rating levels that have been developed to reflect the program's risk thresholds.

Once established, the program risk management strategy drives consistency and effectiveness in program risk management activities throughout the program as part of program integration (Section 7.2.2) and supporting activities (Section 8). In addition, the established program risk management strategy enables the program to communicate and manage program risks consistently throughout the course of the program performance as part of governance (see Section 6.1.6).

Program Strategy Alignment, therefore, is a program performance domain that is initiated during the program definition phase with the development of the business case, program charter, and program roadmap, supported with inputs from environmental assessments and program risk management strategy. This upstream effort results in the development of a program management plan that is aligned with organizational goals and objectives.

4

PROGRAM BENEFITS MANAGEMENT

Program Benefits Management is the performance domain that defines, creates, maximizes, and delivers the benefits provided by the program.

This section includes:

4.1 Benefits Identification

4.2 Benefits Analysis and Planning

4.3 Benefits Delivery

4.4 Benefits Transition

4.5 Benefits Sustainment

Program Benefits Management comprises a number of elements that are central to program success. Program Benefits Management includes processes to clarify the program's planned benefits and intended outcomes and includes processes for monitoring the program's ability to deliver against these benefits and outcomes.

The purpose of Program Benefits Management is to focus program stakeholders (program sponsors, program manager, project managers, program team, program steering committee, and others) on the outcomes and benefits to be provided by the various activities conducted during the program's duration. To do this, the program manager employs Program Benefits Management in order to continually:

◆ Identify and assess the value and impact of program benefits,

◆ Monitor the interdependencies among the outputs being delivered by the various components within the program and how those outputs contribute overall to the program's benefits,

◆ Analyze the potential impact of planned program changes on the expected benefits and outcomes,

◆ Align the expected benefits with the organization's goals and objectives, and

◆ Assign responsibility and accountability for the realization of benefits provided by the program and ensure that the benefits can be sustained.

A benefit is the gains and assets realized by the organization and other stakeholders as the result of outcomes delivered by the program. Some benefits are relatively certain, easily quantifiable, and may include concrete or finite conditions, such as the achievement of an organization's financial objectives (e.g., a 20 % increase in revenue or gross margin) or the creation of a physical product or service for consumption or utility. Other benefits may be less easily quantifiable and may produce somewhat uncertain outcomes. Examples of less certain program outcomes may include an improvement in employee morale or customer satisfaction or may include a benefit such as the reduced incidence of a health condition or disease.

Various types of benefits may be defined and generated by programs. Some benefits, such as expanded market presence, improved financial performance, or operational efficiencies, may be realized by the sponsoring organization while other program outcomes may be realized as benefits by the organization's customers or the program's intended beneficiaries. Regulatory changes may require the initiation of a program. The realized benefits from regulatory compliance programs may be harder to identify. These benefits may be limited to compliance, avoidance of fines, and avoidance of adverse publicity.

Customers and beneficiaries may be operational or functional areas within the performing organization or customers and beneficiaries external to the performing organization, such as a specific group of interested parties, a business sector, an industry, a particular demographic, or the general population.

Benefits are often defined in the context of the intended beneficiary and may be shared among multiple stakeholders. While the organization's customers or the program's intended beneficiaries may be improved in some way as a result of the program, the performing organization may also benefit from the new or improved capability to consistently deliver and sustain the resulting products, services, or capabilities produced.

Other organizations, stakeholders, and intended beneficiaries may not realize a benefit from the program and may be subject to negative impacts, such as a reduction in personnel or consolidation of positions or organizations. Minimizing the negative impacts is as important as realizing the benefits and should be managed, measured, and properly communicated to the organization's leadership and to affected stakeholders and organizations. The program manager should consider coordinating with internal organizations such as the legal, marketing, and human resources departments when addressing a negative consequence.

Programs and their components deliver outcomes that provide benefits that support the organization's strategic goals and objectives. Benefits may not be realized until the completion of the program (or well after completion) or may be realized in an iterative fashion as the components within the program produce incremental results that can be leveraged by the intended recipients. Following program closure, benefits may continue to be realized.

Depending on the nature of the program, the program roadmap is a graphical representation of the incremental benefits and provides a visual of when the return on investment may help fund the future program benefits and outcomes. It is important that, as incremental benefits are being produced, the intended recipients, whether internal or external to the organization, are prepared for the resulting change and are able to sustain the incremental benefits through the completion of the program and beyond.

Some programs deliver benefits only after all of the components have been completed. In this case, the components' deliverables and outcomes all contribute to the full realization of the full benefit. Examples of programs that deliver the intended benefits at the end of the program may include major construction efforts; public works programs, such as roads, dams, or bridges; aerospace programs; aircraft manufacturing or shipbuilding; or medical devices and pharmaceuticals.

Program Benefits Management also ensures that the benefits provided by the organization's investment in a program can be sustained following the conclusion of the program. Throughout the program delivery phase (see Section 7.1.3), program components are planned, developed, integrated, and managed to facilitate the delivery of the intended program benefits. During the program benefits delivery phase, the benefits analysis and planning activities, along with the benefits delivery activities, may be performed in an iterative fashion, especially when corrective action is required to achieve the program benefits.

Program benefits should be monitored and managed. Benefits should be considered an essential part of the program's deliverables. A risk structure for the benefits needs to be established based on the organization's risk appetite and the program's strategic value. Each program benefit needs to be assigned a risk probability. Several factors may drive the probability, including the number of components needed to realize the benefit or the ability of the organization to absorb the change and sustain it.

Program Benefits Management requires continuous interaction with the other performance domains throughout the program's duration. Interactions are cyclical in nature and generally begin top-down during early phases of the program and bottom-up in later phases. For example, Program Strategy Alignment, in conjunction with Program Stakeholder Engagement, provides the critical inputs/parameters to the program, including vision, mission, strategic goals and objectives, and the business case that defines the program benefits. Program performance data are evaluated through program governance to ensure that the program will produce its intended benefits and outcomes.

Figure 4-1 shows the relationship between the program life cycle (see Section 7) and the Program Benefits Management Performance Domain.

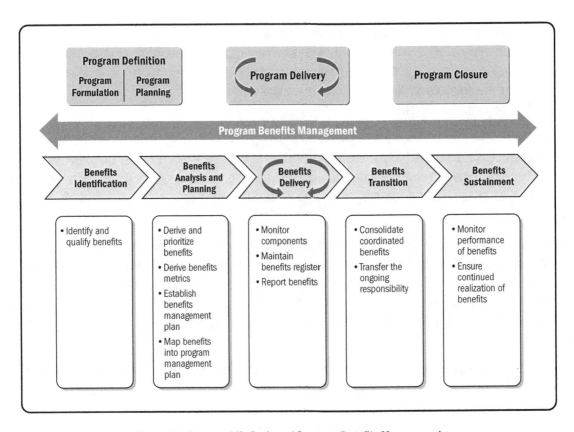

Figure 4-1. Program Life Cycle and Program Benefits Management

4.1 BENEFITS IDENTIFICATION

The purpose of the benefits identification phase is to analyze the available information about organizational and business strategies, internal and external influences, and program drivers to identify and qualify the benefits that program stakeholders expect to realize. As described in Section 3.1, organizational initiatives are identified and documented during an organization's strategic planning exercise. These initiatives describe the goals and activities for the organization. A strategic decision-making body, typically in the form of a program steering committee, may issue a program charter defining the strategic objectives that the program is intended to address and the benefits that are expected to be realized. The program charter is supported by a valid business case. Activities that make up benefits identification include defining the objectives and critical success factors for the program, and identifying and quantifying business benefits.

The business case serves as a formal declaration of the program benefits, the expected delivery, and the justification for the resources that will be expended to deliver it. The business case establishes the authority, intent, philosophy of the business need, and program sponsorship, while providing direction for structure, guiding principles, and organization of the program. The program's business case connects with the organizational strategy and objectives and helps identify the level of investment and support required to achieve the program benefits. See Sections 3.1, 6.1.3, and 7.1.2.1 for further information on the program business case.

4.1.1 BENEFITS REGISTER

The benefits register collects and lists the planned benefits for the program and is used to measure and communicate the delivery of benefits throughout the duration of the program. In the benefits identification phase, the benefits register is developed based on the program business case, the organization's strategic plan, and other relevant program objectives. The register is then reviewed with key stakeholders to develop the appropriate performance measures for each of the benefits. Key performance indicators are identified in this phase and their associated quantitative and qualitative measures are defined and elaborated in the next phase, where the program benefits register is updated. The benefits register may take many forms, but typically includes (at a minimum):

◆ List of planned benefits;

◆ Mapping of the planned benefits to the program components, as reflected in the program roadmap;

◆ Description of how each benefit will be measured;

◆ Key performance indicators and thresholds for evaluating their achievement;

◆ Risk assessment and probability for achieving the benefit;

◆ Status or progress indicator for each benefit;

◆ Target dates and milestones for benefits achievement;

◆ Person, group, or organization responsible for delivering each benefit;

◆ Establishment of processes for measuring progress against the benefits plan; and

◆ Tracking and communications processes necessary to record program progress and report to stakeholders.

4.2 BENEFITS ANALYSIS AND PLANNING

The purpose of the benefits analysis and planning phase is to establish the program benefits management plan and develop the benefits metrics and framework for monitoring and controlling both the components and the measurement of benefits within the program. Activities that make up benefits analysis and planning include:

◆ Establishing the benefits management plan that will guide the work through the remainder of the program,

◆ Defining and prioritizing program components and their interdependencies,

◆ Defining the key performance indicators and associated quantitative measures required to effectively monitor the delivery of program benefits,

◆ Establishing the performance baseline for the program and communicating program performance metrics to the key stakeholders, and

◆ Updating positive and negative risks to benefits as more information becomes known.

It is especially important to quantify the incremental delivery of benefits so that the full realization of planned benefits can be measured during the performance of the program. Meaningful measures help the program manager and stakeholders determine whether benefits exceed their control thresholds and whether they are delivered in a timely manner. Quantification of incremental benefits includes the timing of the delivery of benefits (e.g., the date when realization should start); qualification of intangible benefits (e.g., improved morale or perception of the organization); quantification of the resulting benefits (e.g., hours saved, profit increased, and objectives achieved; cultural, political, or legislative improvement attained; market share increased, competitor strength reduced, or incremental productivity improvements attained); and costs, as illustrated in Figure 4-2. In this example, program costs may continue after program closeout as operational costs to sustain the benefits included in the program funding; program costs may also end at program closeout. When the program continues, it may or may not provide additional funds to the organization accepting the benefit to cover the deferred costs of new benefits; in some cases, the organization may have to self-fund the costs. In addition, quantifiable benefits have not yet exceeded program costs in this example; program benefits are expected to exceed program costs over the time, as specified in the business case.

As the program's benefits are further defined, risks to the program benefits should be further refined and new benefit risks quantified. Examples of risks to implementing benefits include stakeholder acceptance, transition complexity, the amount of change being absorbed by the organization, realization of unexpected outcomes, and other situations that specific industries may encounter. Positive risks in the form of opportunities to optimize the delivery of benefits should also be identified, refined, and quantified. Opportunities may include optimization of how critical resources are allocated or consumed by the program components or leveraging a new technology to reduce the effort or resources required to deliver a particular benefit.

The program governance function helps the program team determine if benefits achievement is occurring within the stated parameters so changes to the components or the program as a whole may be proposed when necessary. This analysis requires linking benefits to program objectives, financial expenditures (operational and capital), measurement criteria (including key performance indicators), and measurement and review points. The benefits management plan is also used during the benefits delivery phase to verify that benefits are being realized as planned, while providing feedback to program stakeholders and the program steering committee to facilitate successful benefit delivery.

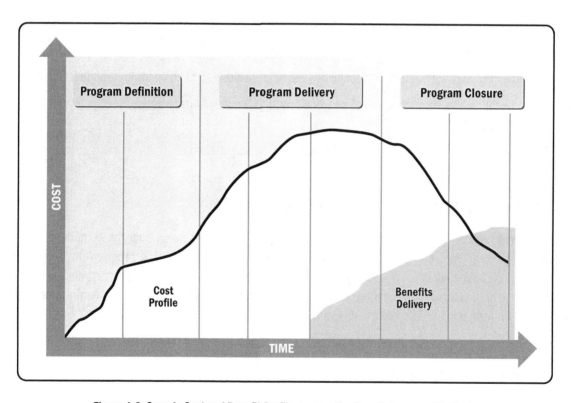

Figure 4-2. Sample Cost and Benefit Profiles across the Generic Program Life Cycle

4.2.1 BENEFITS MANAGEMENT PLAN

The benefits management plan is the documented explanation defining the processes for creating, maximizing, and sustaining the benefits provided by a project or program. The benefits management plan formally documents the activities necessary for achieving the program's planned benefits. It identifies how and when benefits are expected to be delivered to the organization and specifies mechanisms that should be in place to ensure that the benefits are fully realized over time. The benefits management plan is the baseline document that guides the delivery of benefits during the program's performance. The benefits management plan also identifies the associated activities, processes, and systems needed for the change driven by the realization of benefits; the required changes to existing processes and systems; and how and when the transition to an operational state will occur.

The benefits management plan should:

◆ Define each benefit and associated assumptions and determine how each benefit will be achieved;

◆ Link components outputs to the planned program outcomes;

◆ Define the metrics (including key performance indicators) and procedures to measure benefits;

◆ Define roles and responsibilities required to manage the benefits;

◆ Define how the resulting benefits and capabilities will be transitioned into an operational state to achieve benefits;

◆ Define how the resulting capabilities will be transitioned to the individuals, groups, or organizations responsible for sustaining the benefits; and

◆ Provide a process for managing the overall benefits management effort.

4.2.2 BENEFITS MANAGEMENT AND THE PROGRAM ROADMAP

Program benefits management establishes the program architecture that maps how the components will deliver the capabilities and outcomes that are intended to achieve the program benefits. The program roadmap defines the structure of the program components by identifying the relationships among the components and the rules that govern their inclusion. The program roadmap describes evolving aspects of the program including incremental benefits delivery. See Section 3.3 for further information on the program roadmap.

4.2.3 BENEFITS REGISTER UPDATE

The benefits register, initiated during benefits identification, is updated during benefits analysis and planning. At this time, program benefits are mapped to the program components based on the program roadmap. The benefits register is then reviewed with the appropriate stakeholders to define and approve key performance indicators and other measures that will be used to monitor program performance.

4.3 BENEFITS DELIVERY

The purpose of the benefits delivery phase is to ensure that the program delivers the expected benefits, as defined in the benefits management plan. As the program is implemented, risks affecting benefits may be realized, may need to be updated, or may become obsolete; additionally, new risks and updated ones should be included in the benefits register with the associated benefits. Activities that make up benefits delivery include:

◆ Monitoring the organizational environment (including internal and external factors), program objectives, and benefits realization to ensure that the program remains aligned with the organization's strategic objectives;

◆ Initiating, performing, transitioning, and closing components, and managing the interdependencies among them;

◆ Evaluating opportunities and threats affecting benefits, including updating the benefits register for new opportunities and risks affecting benefits, and updating realized or obsolete risks affecting benefits;

◆ Evaluating key performance indicators related to program financials, compliance, quality, safety, and stakeholder satisfaction in order to monitor the delivery of benefits; and

◆ Recording program progress in the benefits register and reporting to key stakeholders as directed in the program communications management plan.

The benefits delivery phase ensures that there is a defined set of reports or metrics reported to the program management office, program steering committee, program sponsors, and other program stakeholders. By consistently monitoring and reporting on benefits metrics, stakeholders can assess the overall health of the program and take appropriate action to ensure successful benefits delivery.

Benefits management is an iterative process. Benefits analysis and planning and benefits delivery, in particular, have a cyclical relationship. Benefits analysis and planning may be continuously revisited as conditions change. Corrective action may need to be taken in response to information gained from monitoring the organizational environment. Components may have to be modified in order to maintain alignment of the expected program results with the organization's strategic objectives. Corrective action may also need to be taken as a result of evaluating program risks and key performance indicators. Components may require modification due to performance related to program financials, compliance, quality, safety, and/or stakeholder satisfaction. These corrective actions may require that program components be added, changed, or terminated during the benefits delivery phase.

4.3.1 BENEFITS AND PROGRAM COMPONENTS

Each component should be initiated at the appropriate time in the program and integrated to incorporate its output to the program as a whole. The initiation and closure of these components are significant milestones in the program roadmap and schedule. The milestones signal the achievement and delivery of incremental benefits. As the benefits management plan is modified to reflect changes in program pacing, the program roadmap (see Section 3.3) is also updated.

4.3.2 BENEFITS AND PROGRAM GOVERNANCE

For a benefit to have value, it needs to be realized to a sufficient degree and in a timely manner. The actual benefits delivered by the program components or program itself should be regularly evaluated against the expected benefits, as defined in the benefits management plan. A key aspect to consider is whether program components, and even the program as a whole, are still viable. Should the program's benefit proposition change (for example, if the overall life cycle cost exceeds the proposed benefits) or if the benefits are delivered too late (for example, when a window of opportunity no longer exists), the program's roadmap should be assessed. Opportunities to optimize the program pacing may also be identified, as well as other synergies and efficiencies among components. The benefits management plan may have to be modified to reflect changes in the program components and pacing. When the benefits management plan is modified, the program roadmap should be updated as well.

The Program Governance Performance Domain integrates with the Benefits Management Performance Domain to help ensure that the program is continuously aligned with the organizational strategy and that the intended value can still be achieved by the delivery of program benefits.

Effective governance helps ensure that the promised outcomes are achieved and delivered for the organization to realize intended benefits. The resulting benefits review requires analysis of the planned versus actual benefits across a wide range of factors, including the key performance indicators. In particular, the following aspects should be analyzed and assessed during the benefits delivery phase:

◆ **Strategic alignment.** Focuses on ensuring the linkage of enterprise and program plans; on defining, maintaining, and validating the program value proposition; and on aligning program management with enterprise operations management. For internally focused programs, the benefits realization processes measure how the new benefits affect the flow of operations of the organization as the change is introduced and how negative impacts and the potential disruptiveness of introducing the change may be minimized.

◆ **Value delivery.** Focuses on ensuring that the program delivers the intended benefits. There may be a window of opportunity for the realization of a particular planned benefit and for that benefit to generate real value. The program manager, program steering committee, and key stakeholders may determine if the window of opportunity was met or compromised by actual events in the program or components (for example, a delay, cost overrun, or scope reduction). Investments may also have time value, where shifts in component schedules have additional financial impact.

4.4 BENEFITS TRANSITION

The purpose of the benefits transition phase is to ensure that program benefits are transitioned to operational areas and can be sustained once they are transferred. Value is delivered when the organization, community, or other program beneficiaries are able to utilize these benefits.

Activities that make up benefits transition include:

◆ Verifying that the integration, transition, and closure of the program and its components meet or exceed the benefit realization criteria established to achieve the program's strategic objectives; and

◆ Developing a transition plan to facilitate the ongoing realization of benefits when turned over to the impacted operational areas.

Benefits transition ensures that the scope of the transition is defined, the stakeholders in the receiving organizations or functions are identified and participate in the planning, the program benefits are measured and sustainment plans are developed, and the transition is executed.

Benefits transition planning activities within the program are only one part of the complete transition process. The receiving organization or function is responsible for all preparation processes and activities within their domain to ensure that the product, service, or capability is received and incorporated into their domain. There may be multiple transition events as individual program components close or as other work activity within the program closes.

Benefits may be realized before the formal work of the program has ended and will likely continue long after the formal work has been completed. Benefits transition may be performed following the close of an individual program component if that component is intended to provide incremental benefits to the organization. Benefits transition may also occur following the close of the overall program when the program as a whole is intended to provide benefits to the organization and no incremental benefits have been identified.

Benefits are quantified so that their realization can be measured over time. Benefits are sometimes not realized until long after the end of active work on a program and may need to be monitored well after the program has closed. At the end of the program, the resulting benefits should be compared against those intended in the business case to ensure that the program will actually deliver the intended benefits.

Benefits transition activities ensure that individual program component results or outputs meet acceptance criteria, are satisfactorily closed or integrated into other program elements, and contribute to the overall achievement of the collective set of program benefits. Benefits transition activities may include but are not limited to:

- ◆ Evaluation of program and program component performance against applicable acceptance criteria, including key performance indicators;

- ◆ Review and evaluation of acceptance criteria applicable to delivered components or outputs;

- ◆ Review of operational and program process documentation;

- ◆ Review of training and maintenance materials (if they apply);

- ◆ Review of applicable contractual agreements;

- ◆ Assessment to determine if resulting changes have been successfully integrated;

- ◆ Activities related to improving acceptance of resulting changes (workshops, meetings, training, etc.);

- ◆ Transfer of risk(s) affecting the benefits transitioned to the receiving organization;

- ◆ Readiness assessment and approval by the receiving person, group, or organization; and

- ◆ Disposition of all related resources.

The receiver in the transition process varies depending on the individual component event and program type. A product support organization could be the receiver for a product line that a company develops. For a service provided to customers, the receiver could be the service management organization. If the work products are developed for an external customer, the transition could be to the customer's organization. In some cases, the transition may be from one program to another.

A program may also be terminated with no transition to operations. This may occur when the charter is fulfilled and operations are not necessary to continue realization of ongoing benefits, or the chartered program is no longer of value to the organization. Transition may be a formal activity among functions within a single organization or a contract-based activity with an entity outside the organization. The receiving entity should have a clear understanding of the capabilities or results to be transitioned and what is required for the entity to successfully sustain the benefits. All pertinent documents, training and materials, supporting systems, facilities, and personnel are typically provided during the transition and may include transition meetings and conferences.

Should any remaining risk(s) affecting the transitioned benefit remain open, the program manager should transfer the risk to the appropriate organization. The organization accepting the benefit may not be the team to monitor ongoing risk for the benefit. The risk(s) may be monitored by a governance organization such as a program management office (PMO).

4.5 BENEFITS SUSTAINMENT

The purpose of the benefits sustainment phase is the ongoing maintenance activities performed beyond the end of the program by receiving organizations to ensure continued generation of the improvements and outcomes delivered by the program. As the program is closed, responsibility for sustaining the benefits provided by the program may pass to another organization or another program. Benefits may be sustained through operations, maintenance, new components, or other efforts. A benefits sustainment plan should be developed prior to program closure to identify the risks, processes, measures, metrics, and tools necessary to ensure the continued realization of the benefits delivered.

Ongoing sustainment of program benefits should be planned by the program manager and the component project managers during the performance of the program. The actual work that ensures the sustainment of benefits is typically conducted after the close of the program and is beyond the scope of the individual components. Although the receiving person, organization, or beneficiary group performs the work that ensures benefits continue beyond the end of the program, the program manager is responsible for planning these post-transition activities during the performance of the program.

The responsibility for benefits sustainment falls outside the traditional project life cycle; however, this responsibility may remain within the program life cycle. While these ongoing product, service, or capability support activities may fall within the scope of the program, they typically are operational in nature and typically are not run as a program or project.

Activities that make up benefits sustainment include but are not limited to:

◆ Planning for the operational, financial, and behavioral changes necessary for program recipients (individuals, groups, organizations, industries, and sectors) to continue monitoring performance;

◆ Implementing the required change efforts to ensure that the capabilities provided during the course of the program continue when the program is closed and the program's resources are returned to the organization;

◆ Monitoring the performance of the product, service, capability, or results from a reliability and availability-for-use perspective and comparing actual performance to planned performance, including key performance indicators;

◆ Monitoring the continued suitability of the deployed product, service, capability, or results to provide the benefits expected by the customers owning and operating it. This may include the continued viability of interfaces with other products, services, capabilities, or results and the continued completeness of the functionality;

◆ Monitoring the continued availability of logistics support for the product, service, capability, or results in light of technological advancements and the willingness of vendors to continue to support older configurations;

◆ Responding to customer inputs on their needs for product, service, capability, or results of support assistance or for improvements in performance or functionality;

◆ Providing on-demand support for the product, service, capability, or results either in features, improved technical information, or real-time help desk support;

◆ Planning for and establishing operational support of the product, service, capability, or results separate from the program management function without relinquishing the other product support functions;

◆ Updating technical information concerning the product, service, capability, or improvement in response to frequent product support queries;

◆ Planning the transition of product or capability support from program management to an operations function within an organization;

◆ Planning the retirement and phase-out of the product or capability, or the cessation of support with appropriate guidance to the current customers;

◆ Developing business cases and the potential initiation of new projects or programs to respond to operational issues with the deployed product, service, or capability being supported or public acceptance/reaction to the improvement or to legislative changes; political, economic, and socioeconomic changes; cultural shifts; or logistics issues with a deployed product, service, capability, or results being supported; and

◆ Monitoring any outstanding risks affecting the program's benefits.

Refer to Figure 1-1 for further information regarding program life cycle and benefits.

5

PROGRAM STAKEHOLDER ENGAGEMENT

Program Stakeholder Engagement is the performance domain that identifies and analyzes stakeholder needs and manages expectations and communications to foster stakeholder support.

This section includes:

5.1 Program Stakeholder Identification

5.2 Program Stakeholder Analysis

5.3 Program Stakeholder Engagement Planning

5.4 Program Stakeholder Engagement

5.5 Program Stakeholder Communications

A stakeholder is an individual, group, or organization that may affect, be affected by, or perceive itself to be affected by a decision, activity, or outcome of a project, program, or portfolio.

Stakeholders may be internal or external to the program and may have a positive or negative impact on the outcome of the program. Program and project managers need to be aware of the stakeholders' impact and level of influence to understand and address the changing environments of programs and projects.

Stakeholders should be identified, analyzed, categorized, and monitored. Unlike program resources, not all stakeholders can be managed directly—but their expectations can be. In many cases, external stakeholders have more influence than the program manager, the program team, and even the program sponsor. Balancing stakeholder interests is important, considering their potential impact on program benefits realization or the inherent conflicting nature of those interests. People have a tendency to resist direct management when the relationship does not have a hierarchical affiliation. For this reason, most program management literature focuses on the notion of *stakeholder engagement* rather than *stakeholder management*.

Stakeholder engagement is often expressed as direct and indirect communication among the stakeholder and the program's leaders and team. Engagement with the program team may be performed by people with different roles in the program and project teams. Stakeholder engagement, however, includes more than just communication. For example, stakeholders can be engaged by involving them in goal setting, quality analysis reviews, or other program activities. The primary objective is to gain and maintain stakeholder buy-in for the program's objectives, benefits, and outcomes.

Ambiguity and uncertainty are common characteristics of programs. The complexity of those environments warrants the efforts of the program manager to understand and manage the wide stakeholder base. Figure 5-1 depicts a diverse stakeholder environment that may shape the actions needed to manage those expectations. Mapping stakeholders is a pivotal step to ensure successful expectation management, and in turn deliver business benefits to the organization. Beyond the communications aspect, stakeholder engagement concerns negotiation of objectives, agreement on desired benefits, commitment to resources, and ongoing support throughout the program.

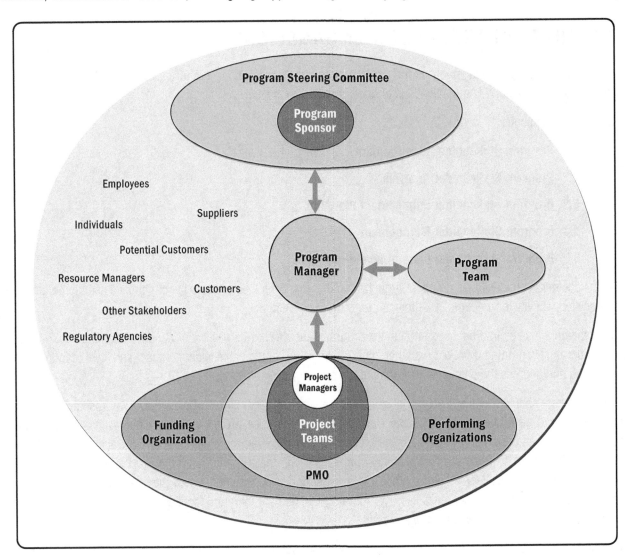

Figure 5-1. Stakeholder Environment for Programs

The level of interest and the level of influence in the program may vary widely from stakeholder to stakeholder. A stakeholder may be unaware of the program or, if aware, may not support it. It is the responsibility of the program manager to expend sufficient time and energy with known stakeholders to ensure all points of view have been considered and addressed.

The program manager interacts with stakeholders in the following ways:

◆ Engages stakeholders by assessing their attitudes and interests toward the program and their change readiness;

◆ Includes stakeholders in program activities and uses communications targeted to their needs, interests, requirements, expectations, and wants, according to their change readiness and selected organizational change management strategy speed and scale;

◆ Monitors stakeholder feedback within the context and understanding of the relationship to the program; and

◆ Supports training initiatives as needed within the context of the program or related organizational structure of the program component.

This two-way communication enables the program manager to deliver the benefits for the organization in accordance with the program charter.

Stakeholder engagement at the program level can be challenging because some stakeholders view the program benefits as change. People have the propensity to resist change whenever they have not directly requested it, have not participated in creating it, do not understand the necessity for it, or are concerned with the effect of the change on them personally. Thus, the program manager and the program team members need to understand the attitudes and the agendas for each stakeholder throughout the duration of the program. The program manager should be the champion for change in the organization and understand the motivations of each stakeholder who could attempt to alter the course of the program or intentionally derail it and prevent the program from realizing one or more of its intended benefits or outcomes. As the program evolves in this complex environment and it adapts to ensure that it delivers its intended benefits, its strategy and plans may change. For support, the program manager also draws on the program sponsor or sponsoring group to foster organizational conditions, through program governance, to enable the effective realization of program benefits.

The program manager needs to bridge the gap between the current state of the organization and the desired future state. To do so, the program manager should understand the current state and how the program and its benefits will move the organization to the future state. Therefore, the program manager should be familiar with organizational change management.

Successful program managers utilize strong leadership skills to set clear stakeholder engagement goals for the program team to address the change the program will bring. These goals include engaging stakeholders to assess their readiness for change, planning for the change, providing program resources and support for the change, facilitating or negotiating the approach to implement change, and obtaining and evaluating the stakeholders' feedback on the program's progress.

5.1 PROGRAM STAKEHOLDER IDENTIFICATION

Program stakeholder identification aims to systematically identify all key stakeholders (or stakeholder groups) in the stakeholder register. This register lists the stakeholders and categorizes their relationship to the program, their ability to influence the program outcome, their degree of support for the program, and other characteristics or attributes the program manager feels could influence the stakeholders' perception and the program's outcomes.

Table 5-1 provides an example of stakeholder categorization within a program.

Table 5-1. Stakeholder Register

Name	Organizational Position	Program Role	Support Level	Influence	Communication	Other Characteristics
Stakeholder 1	Director	Supplier	Neutral	Low	Email monthly	Interests
Stakeholder 2	Customer	Recipient	Supportive	Medium	Conference weekly	Needs
Stakeholder 3	Sr. Vice President	Sponsor	Leading	High	Status report quarterly	Status—engaged

The stakeholder register should be established and maintained in such a way that members of the program team can reference it easily for use in reporting, distributing program deliverables, and providing formal and informal communications. It should be noted that the stakeholder register may contain politically and legally sensitive information, and may have access and review restrictions placed on it by the program manager. As a result, it may be appropriate to ensure that the stakeholder register is appropriately secured. The program manager should comply with data privacy regulations in countries where the program operates. The stakeholder register is a dynamic document. As the program evolves, new stakeholders may emerge or interests of current groups may shift. The program manager should monitor the environment, and prepare and update the register as required.

Examples of key program stakeholders include but are not limited to:

◆ **Program sponsor.** An individual or a group that provides resources and support for the program and is accountable for enabling success. The program sponsor is often the champion of the program.

◆ **Program steering committee.** A group of participants representing various program-related interests with the purpose of supporting the program under its authority by providing guidance, endorsements, and approvals through the governance practices. This committee may be referred to as the program governance board.

◆ **Portfolio manager.** The person or group assigned by the performing organization to establish, balance, monitor, and control portfolio components in order to achieve strategic business objectives.

◆ **Program manager.** The individual authorized by the performing organization to lead the team or teams responsible for achieving program objectives.

◆ **Project manager.** The person assigned by the performing organization to lead the team that is responsible for achieving project objectives.

◆ **Program team members.** The individuals performing program activities.

◆ **Project team members.** The individuals performing constituent project activities.

◆ **Funding organization.** The part of the organization or the external organization providing funding for the program.

◆ **Performing organization.** The organization whose personnel are the most directly involved in doing the work of the project or program.

◆ **Program management office.** A management structure that standardizes the program-related governance processes and facilitates the sharing of resources, methodologies, tools, and techniques.

◆ **Customers.** The individual or organization that will use the new capabilities delivered by the program and derive the anticipated benefits. The customer is a major stakeholder in the program's final result and will influence whether the program is judged to be successful or not.

◆ **Potential customers.** The past and future customers who will be watching intently to see how well the program delivers the stated benefits.

◆ **Suppliers.** Product and service providers who are often affected by changing policies and procedures.

◆ **Regulatory agencies.** A public authority or government agency responsible for setting and managing the regulatory and legal boundaries of their local and national sovereign governments. Typically, these organizations will set mandatory standards or requirements.

- **Affected individuals or organizations.** Those who perceive that they will either benefit from or be disadvantaged by the program's activities.

- **Other groups.** Groups representing consumer, environmental, or other interests (including political interests). Organizational support functions such as human resources, legal, administration, and infrastructure are also considered key stakeholders.

The identification of stakeholders using the brainstorming technique aims to name stakeholders across the entire program life cycle. The resulting stakeholder register is an essential tool leading to effective engagement.

5.2 PROGRAM STAKEHOLDER ANALYSIS

Once all major stakeholders are listed in the stakeholder register, the program manager will categorize them in order to start analyzing them. The categorization will highlight differences in their needs, expectations, or influence. Key information should be obtained from stakeholders in order to better understand the organizational culture, politics, and concerns related to the program, as well as the overall impact of the program. This information may be obtained through historical information, individual interviews, focus groups, or questionnaires and surveys. Questionnaires and surveys allow the program team to solicit feedback from a greater number of stakeholders than is possible with interviews or focus groups. Regardless of the technique used, key information should be gathered through open-ended questions to elicit stakeholder feedback. From the information gathered, a prioritized list of stakeholders should be developed to help focus the engagement effort on the people and organizations who have the most influence (positive or negative) on the program. The program manager should establish a balance between activities related to mitigating the effect of stakeholders who view the program negatively and encouraging the active support of stakeholders who see the program as a positive contribution.

For complex programs, the program manager may develop a stakeholder map to visually represent the interaction of all stakeholders' current and desired support and influence. The map serves as a tool to assess the impact of a change on the program community. It allows the program team to make informed decisions about how and when to engage stakeholders, taking into account their interest, influence, involvement, interdependencies and support levels. An alternative classification model used for stakeholder analysis is the power/interest grid. It groups stakeholders based on their level of authority ("power") and their level of concern ("interest") regarding the project outcomes. Figure 5-2 presents an example of the power/ interest grid with A-H representing the placement of generic stakeholders.

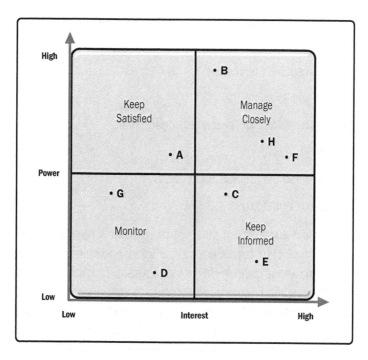

Figure 5-2. Example Power/Interest Grid with Stakeholders

By identifying stakeholder expectations and clearly outlining key indicators and expected benefits, the program manager creates a framework to address ongoing program activities and evolving stakeholder needs. The stakeholder map can function as a tool to help identify the need for interactions with stakeholders. It brings to light the potential partnerships among stakeholders and the collaboration opportunities that contribute to the success of the program. As the need arises, the program manager can use the stakeholder map to remind teams of which stakeholders need to be engaged at various times in the program life cycle. The overall stakeholder register and the prioritization of stakeholder engagement activities should be regularly reviewed and updated as the work of the program progresses.

5.3 PROGRAM STAKEHOLDER ENGAGEMENT PLANNING

The stakeholder engagement planning activity outlines how all program stakeholders will be engaged throughout the duration of the program. The stakeholder register and stakeholder map are analyzed with consideration of the organization's strategic plan, the program charter, and program business case to understand the environment in which the program will operate.

As part of the stakeholder analysis and engagement planning, the following aspects for each stakeholder are taken into consideration:

◆ Organizational culture and acceptance of change,

◆ Attitudes about the program and its sponsors,

◆ Relevant phase(s) applicable to stakeholders specific engagement,

◆ Expectation of program benefits delivery,

◆ Degree of support or opposition to the program benefits, and

◆ Ability to influence the outcome of the program.

This effort results in the stakeholder engagement plan, which contains a detailed strategy for effective stakeholder engagement, based on current situation. The plan includes stakeholder engagement guidelines and provides insight on how the stakeholders are engaged in various components of the program. The plan defines the metrics used to measure the performance of stakeholder engagement activities. This could include measures of participation in meetings and other communication channels, and the degree of active or passive support or resistance, and can also strive to measure the effectiveness of the engagement in meeting its intended goal. The guidelines for stakeholder engagement should be provided to the component projects, subsidiary programs, and other program activities under the program. The stakeholder engagement plan provides critical information used in the development of program documentation and its ongoing alignment as the known stakeholders change (see Section 8.1.2.2).

5.4 PROGRAM STAKEHOLDER ENGAGEMENT

Stakeholder engagement is a continuous program activity because the list of stakeholders and their attitudes and opinions change as the program progresses and delivers benefits. One of the primary roles of the program manager throughout the duration of the program is to ensure all stakeholders are adequately and appropriately engaged. Identifying stakeholders, mapping their interests, and planning for stakeholder engagement directly support this process. The stakeholder register, stakeholder map, and stakeholder engagement plan should be referenced and evaluated often, and updated as needed.

Interacting and engaging with stakeholders allows the program team to communicate program benefits and their relevance to the organization's strategic objectives. When necessary, the program manager may utilize strong communication, negotiation, and conflict resolution skills to help defuse stakeholder opposition to the program and its stated benefits. Large programs with diverse stakeholders may also require facilitated negotiation sessions among stakeholders or stakeholder groups when their expectations conflict.

To help stakeholders establish common high-level expectations for the delivery of the program's benefits, the program manager provides stakeholders with appropriate information contained in the program charter and program business case, which can include an accompanying executive brief to summarize the details of the risks, dependencies, and benefits.

The primary metrics for stakeholder engagement are positive contributions to the realization of the program's objectives and benefits, stakeholder participation, and frequency or rate of communication with the program team. The program manager strives to ensure all interactions with the stakeholders are adequately logged, including meeting invitations, attendance, meeting minutes, and action items. Program managers review stakeholder metrics regularly to identify potential risks caused by lack of participation from stakeholders. Participation trends are analyzed and root-cause analysis is performed to identify and address the causes of nonparticipation. The history of stakeholder participation provides important background information that could influence stakeholder perceptions and expectations. For example, when a stakeholder has not been actively participating, it may be that the stakeholder is confident in the program's direction or possibly has inaccurate expectations or has lost interest in the program. Thorough analysis avoids incorrect assumptions about stakeholder behavior that could lead to unanticipated issues or poor program management decisions.

As the program team works with the stakeholders, it collects and logs stakeholder issues and concerns and manages them to closure. Use of an issue log to document, prioritize, and track issues helps the entire program team understand the feedback received from the stakeholders. When the list of stakeholders is small, a simple spreadsheet may be an adequate tracking tool. For programs with complex risks and issues affecting large numbers of stakeholders, a more sophisticated tracking and prioritization mechanism may be required.

Stakeholder issues and concerns are likely to affect aspects of the program such as its scope, benefits, risks, costs, schedule, priorities, and outcomes. Impact analysis could be used to understand the urgency and probability of stakeholder issues and determine which issues could turn into program risks.

5.5 PROGRAM STAKEHOLDER COMMUNICATIONS

Effective communications create a bridge between diverse stakeholders who may have different cultural and organizational backgrounds, different levels of expertise, and different perspectives and interests, all of which may impact or influence the delivery of benefits by the program. Communication is at the heart of program stakeholder engagement. It is key to executing program endeavors and, ultimately, delivering benefits to the organization. This critical component is a vehicle for information sharing, negotiation, and collaboration among the program team members to drive program implementation efforts.

The program manager should actively engage stakeholders throughout the life cycle of the program, with particular attention to those key stakeholders who are high in power and influence. A strategy can be crafted for each stakeholder as identified in the stakeholder register (see Table 5-1). This accounts for communication requirements such as what information should be communicated, including language, format, content, and level of detail. It can also address a feedback loop to discuss program changes and an escalation process. The resulting communication approach targets stakeholders' support for the program strategy and delivery of the program benefits.

Some stakeholders are naturally curious about the program and often raise questions. These questions and their answers should be captured and published in a way that allows multiple stakeholders to benefit from the exchange. In many cases, the documentation may need to be formatted and presented differently for certain stakeholder audiences. It is important that decision-making stakeholders are provided with adequate information to make the right decisions at the right time necessary to move the program forward. The program manager should continually monitor changes and update stakeholder engagement activities and deliverables as needed.

Communication with some stakeholders is inherent in many program management activities. These activities are described in detail in Section 8. The program manager should constantly monitor and foster an environment where stakeholder communication needs are met.

6

PROGRAM GOVERNANCE

Program Governance is the performance domain that enables and performs program decision making, establishes practices to support the program, and maintains program oversight.

This section includes:

6.1 Program Governance Practices

6.2 Program Governance Roles

6.3 Program Governance Design and Implementation

Program Governance comprises the framework, functions, and processes by which a program is monitored, managed, and supported in order to meet organizational strategic and operational goals. The focus of program governance is the delivery of program benefits by establishing the systems and methods by which a program and its strategy are defined, authorized, monitored, and supported by its sponsoring organization. A program governance framework, when well designed, provides practices for effective decision making and ensures the program is managed appropriately. Program governance is performed through the actions of a review and decision-making group that is charged with endorsing or approving recommendations regarding a program under its authority. The program manager has management responsibilities to ensure that the program is run within the governance framework while managing the day-to-day program activities. The program manager should ensure that the program team understands and abides by the governance procedures and the underlying governance principles.

Program governance may also refer to the framework, functions, and processes by which a program team monitors and manages the components that are being performed to support the program. Governance of components is often achieved through the actions of the program manager and program team responsible for the integrated outcomes of the program. Such a responsibility may also be called component governance.

Program governance is impacted by organizational governance, which is a structured way to provide control, direction, and coordination through people, policies, and processes to meet organizational strategic and operational goals. Typically, portfolio governance is the hierarchical level of governance where program investments are authorized.

Figure 6-1 illustrates the governance relationships for programs. Within a portfolio structure, portfolio governance-supporting functions and processes are linked to programs through portfolio governance. For stand-alone programs that are outside of a portfolio structure, a governing body provides governance-supporting functions and processes to programs, including governance policies, oversight, control, integration, and decision-making functions and processes. The type and frequency of the governance activities are determined by portfolio governance and governing bodies. The portfolio provides governance policies, oversight, control, integration, and decision-making functions and processes to programs within the portfolio structure.

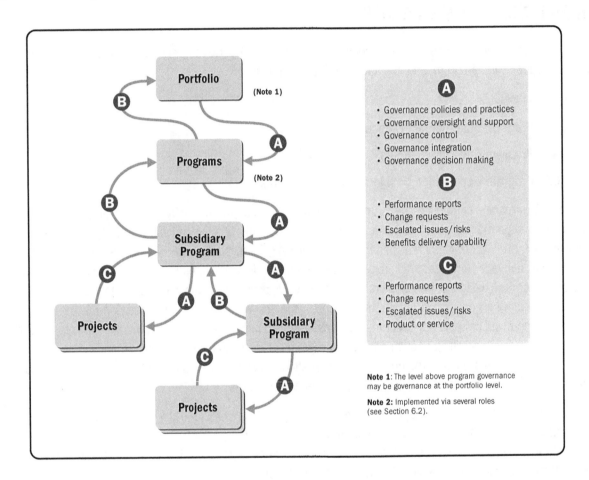

Figure 6-1. Governance Hierarchy

Effective program governance supports the success of a program by:

◆ Ensuring that the goals of the program remain aligned with the strategic vision, operational capabilities, and resource commitments of the sponsoring organization. Compliance with the reporting and controlling processes required to support this alignment is enforced by the Program Governance domain;

◆ Approving, endorsing, and initiating the program and securing funding from the sponsoring organization;

◆ Establishing clear, well-understood agreements as to how the sponsoring organization will oversee the program, and conversely, the degree of autonomy that the program will be given in the pursuit of its goals;

◆ Facilitating the engagement of program stakeholders by establishing clear expectations for each program's interactions with key governing stakeholders throughout the program;

◆ Creating an environment for communicating and addressing program risks and uncertainties to the organization, as well as opportunities and issues that arise during the course of program performance;

◆ Providing a framework that is aligned with portfolio and corporate governance policies and processes for assessing and ensuring the program is compliant. Each program may need to create a particular governance process or procedure, but it should be aligned with the organization's governance principles;

◆ Designing and authorizing the assurance process and, when required, executing reviews and health checks of the program progress in delivering its expected benefits. Various review types are used, including phase-gate reviews, other decision point reviews, and periodic health checks;

◆ Enabling the organization to assess the viability of the organization's strategic plan and the level of support required to achieve it;

◆ Selecting, endorsing, and enabling the pursuit of program components, including projects, subsidiary programs, and other program activities; and

◆ Making decisions to transition between phases, terminate, or close the program.

Effective program governance is especially important in environments that are highly complex or uncertain when it is necessary to respond rapidly to outcomes and information that become available during the course of the program. Program governance makes it possible to clarify the organization's vision, facilitate alignment of the program with organizational strategy, and enable the periodic balancing of program demands with current organizational capabilities. Governance participants are able to monitor and, as necessary, authorize or limit changes to the activities performed as part of a program. Governance decision forums focus on facilitating the adaptive realignment of the program's approach to enable the delivery of intended benefits. The roles and participants performing program governance activities are described in Section 6.2.

Program governance provides an important means by which programs seek authorization and support for dynamically changing program strategies or plans in response to emergent outcomes. A program within a portfolio is likely to be governed within the framework of the portfolio. Portfolio governance provides the framework, functions, and processes providing oversight, control, integration, and decision-making practices to programs, projects, and operations within the portfolio structure. In the event that the organization does not have portfolios of programs and projects, then the process to develop the idea and steps to authorize the program should be carried out within the organizational governance framework.

6.1 PROGRAM GOVERNANCE PRACTICES

6.1.1 PROGRAM GOVERNANCE PLAN

To facilitate the design and implementation of effective governance, many organizations prepare documented descriptions of each program's governance frameworks, functions, and processes. Such descriptions are summarized in a program governance plan, which may be a stand-alone document or a subsection of the program management plan. While typically there will be a program governance plan for each program in the organization, some organizations may use a single program governance plan to govern several programs.

The purpose of the program governance plan is to describe the systems and methods to be used to monitor, manage, and support a given program, and the responsibilities of specific roles for ensuring the timely and effective use of those systems and methods. This plan is referenced throughout the program's duration to ensure the program is conforming to established governance expectations and agreements. The program governance plan may be modified as appropriate, based on outcomes attained during the course of the program. It is generally accepted good practice to ensure that modifications are effectively communicated to those stakeholders responsible for program governance and program management.

6.1.1.1 DEFINITIONS OF ROLES AND RESPONSIBILITIES

The program governance plan describes the structure and composition of the group of governance participants and defines the roles and responsibilities of key stakeholders. The plan defines who will have accountability and authority with respect to key decision-making categories and responsibility boundaries.

6.1.1.2 PLANNED GOVERNANCE MEETINGS

The program governance plan should contain a schedule of anticipated program-related governance meetings, activities, and key milestones, such as scheduled expected decision-point reviews (including phase gate reviews), program health checks, and required audits. It provides guidance for the scheduling of additional governance meetings or activities by defining criteria for their scheduling (for example, the review of program outcomes that may influence the program approach or program resourcing needs). The program governance plan thereby serves to influence the program management plan, defining the program's requirements for governance interactions and review.

6.1.1.3 OTHER CONTENT

In addition to the descriptions and definition in Sections 6.1.1.1 and 6.1.1.2, the following items may also be covered in the program governance plan:

- ◆ **Dependencies, assumptions, and constraints.** List of governance key dependencies, assumptions, and constraints including resource, budget, and operational limitations.

- ◆ **Benefits, performance metrics, and measurement.** List of the methods and metrics used to evaluate the program and evaluate component contributions to benefits, and a description of how information on the components will be collected, consolidated, and reported (e.g., a balanced scorecard or dashboard).

- ◆ **Support services.** Identification of the areas where governance-related support is needed. Included is a description of the feedback and support approach used during the program.

- ◆ **Stakeholder engagement.** A listing of the stakeholders who should be engaged and communicated with during the program's life cycle and governance activities (see Section 5 for more details).

- ◆ **Governance practices.** The intended design and implementation of practices described in Sections 6.1.2 to 6.1.12 will also be covered in the program governance plan.

6.1.2 PROGRAM GOVERNANCE AND VISION AND GOALS

The vision and goals of the organization provide the basis for strategic mandates that drive the definition of most programs. Program governance ensures that any program within its area of authority defines its vision and goals in order to effectively support those of the organization.

6.1.3 PROGRAM APPROVAL, ENDORSEMENT, AND DEFINITION

In most organizations, program governance outlines responsibility for approving each program's approach and plan for how it will pursue program and organizational goals, and for authorizing the use of resources to support components and other program work in pursuit of that approach. These approvals occur in the program definition phase and are facilitated by two program artifacts:

- **Program business case.** Serves as a formal projection of the benefits that the program is expected to deliver and a justification for the resources that will be expended to deliver it. See Section 3.1 for more information on the program business case.

- **Program charter.** Authorizes the program management team to use organizational resources to pursue the program and links the program to its business case and the organization's strategic priorities. See Section 3.2 for more information on the program charter.

Program governance facilitates program funding to the degree necessary to support the approved business case. Often, program funding is provided through a budgetary process that is controlled by a forum responsible for oversight of several programs. In these instances, program funding is provided in a manner consistent with program needs and organizational priorities, as may be defined through the organization's portfolio management processes.

When program funding needs to be secured from external sources, program governance is typically responsible for entering into the appropriate agreements necessary to secure it. The funding may have constraints that limit its use due to law, regulations, or other limitations.

6.1.4 PROGRAM SUCCESS CRITERIA

Governance (which could be at the organizational, portfolio, or program level) establishes the minimum acceptable criteria for a successful program and the methods by which those criteria will be measured, communicated, and endorsed. The criteria describe the definition of success consistent with the expectations and needs of key program stakeholders, and reinforce the program alignment to deliver the maximum attainable benefits.

6.1.5 PROGRAM MONITORING, REPORTING, AND CONTROLLING

The program governance participants are uniquely positioned to monitor the progress of programs in their pursuit of organizational goals, working collaboratively with the program manager to maximize the opportunities for success for the program.

To support the organization's ability to monitor program progress and strengthen the organization's ability to assess program status and conformance with organizational controls, many organizations define standardized reporting and controlling processes applicable to all programs. Program governance assumes responsibility for enforcing program compliance with such processes. Reporting and controlling documents may include:

◆ Operational status and progress of programs, components, and related activities;

◆ Expected or incurred program resource requirements;

◆ Known program risks, their response plans, and escalation criteria;

◆ Strategic and operational assumptions;

◆ Benefits realized and expected sustainment;

◆ Decision criteria, tracking, and communication;

◆ Program change control;

◆ Compliance with corporate and legal policies;

◆ Program information management;

◆ Issues and issue response plans; and

◆ Program funding and financial performance.

6.1.6 PROGRAM RISK AND ISSUE GOVERNANCE

Effective risk and issue management practices ensure that key risks and issues are escalated appropriately and resolved in a timely manner. The escalation processes typically operate at two levels: *(a)* within the program, between component teams, the program management team, and the program steering committee; and *(b)* outside the program, between the program management team, the program's steering committee, and other stakeholders. The expectations for risk and issue escalation at all levels are documented and communicated to ensure that the organization clearly defines its requirements for the engagement of governing stakeholders at the appropriate times for effective risk and issue management.

Based on the risk appetite of the organization, and working with organizational governance and the program management team, program governance may establish program risk thresholds for adherence within the program.

6.1.7 PROGRAM QUALITY GOVERNANCE

The governance of quality is essential to the success of the program. Quality management planning is often performed at the component level and is therefore governed at that level. The governance participants are responsible for reviewing and approving the approach to quality management and the standards by which quality will be measured. In some cases, the governance participants may define such measures, which include:

◆ Minimum quality criteria and standards to be applied to all components of the program;

◆ Minimum requirements for quality planning, quality control, and quality assurance by components;

◆ Any required program-level quality assurance or quality control activities; and

◆ Roles and responsibilities for required program-level quality assurance and quality control activities.

Quality control activities may differ at the component level based on the complexity and uncertainty of the given component. More details of the Program Quality Management activities can be found in Section 8.

6.1.8 PROGRAM CHANGE GOVERNANCE

Program governance plays a critical role in the authorization of changes to the program. The program steering committee is responsible for defining the types of changes that a program manager would be independently authorized to approve and those changes that would be significant enough to require further discussion prior to approval. As a result of the monitoring, reporting, and controlling practices, the governance participants should be well positioned to assess proposed changes to the program's planned approach or activities.

The program manager assesses whether the risks associated with potential changes are acceptable or desirable, whether the proposed changes are operationally feasible and organizationally supportable, and whether the changes are significant enough to require approval of the program steering committee. The program manager then recommends changes that require approval by program governance participants through the program steering committee. The extent to which a change can be authorized by program governance is bounded by the program business case and organizational strategy. A record of the proposed change, its rationale, and its outcome is maintained by the program team. Section 8.2.1 provides details of the program change governance activity.

6.1.9 PROGRAM GOVERNANCE REVIEWS

Program governance endorses reviews of programs at key decision points in the program life cycle. These reviews often are conducted at times that coincide with the initiation or completion of significant segments of a program to enable governance to approve or disapprove the passage of a program from one significant segment to another. They also facilitate the review and approval of any required changes to the program at key decision points.

Key decision points occur at the end of program phases. Phase-gate reviews are reviews at the end of a phase in which a decision is made to continue to the next phase, to continue with modification, or to end a program or program component. These enable governance to approve or disapprove the passage of a program from one significant phase to another.

Program governance endorses decision-point reviews and their specific objectives, which may include assessments of the:

◆ Strategic alignment of the program and its components with the intended goals of both the program and the organization;

◆ Outcomes of a program component's activities, to assess the actual (versus planned) realization of program benefits and the potential need to adapt the program's plan in response to such outcomes;

◆ Risk that the program faces, to ensure that the level of risk remains acceptable and to provide opportunity for program governance to assist in responding to risk;

◆ Program resource needs and organizational commitments in addition to capabilities for fulfilling them;

◆ Stakeholder satisfaction with current program performance;

◆ Potential impact of external (environmental) developments on program strategies and plans;

◆ Program compliance with organizational quality or process standards;

◆ Information critical to strategic prioritization or operational investments of the organization as part of its portfolio management activities;

◆ Issues that should be resolved in order to improve program progress;

◆ Potential need for changes to elements of the program, in order to further improve the program's performance and likelihood of success; and

◆ Fulfillment of criteria for exiting the preceding phase and entering the succeeding phase.

Other reviews may be held to support the decision-making needs of the organization, for example, program reviews held in support of portfolio management or budgeting processes.

Through the conduct of reviews, the program steering committee has the opportunity to confirm its support for continuation of the program as defined or to initiate recommendations for adaptive changes to the program's strategy, improving the program's ability to pursue and deliver its intended benefits.

At times, decision-point reviews may result in termination of the program (for example, when it is determined, for any number of reasons, that the program is not likely to deliver its expected benefits, cannot be supported at the investment level required, or should no longer be pursued as determined in a portfolio review).

The frequency of program reviews and the specific requirements of those reviews may reflect the autonomy given to the program team to oversee and manage the program. The organization's expectations for program governance reviews should be detailed in the program governance plan.

6.1.10 PROGRAM PERIODIC HEALTH CHECKS

Program periodic health checks, generally held between decision-point reviews, assess a program's ongoing performance and progress toward the realization and sustainment of benefits. The importance and use of these reviews increase when there is an extended period between scheduled decision-point reviews. The program governance plan specifies governance requirements for the scheduling, the content, the participants, and the assessments (or metrics) to be used during such health checks.

6.1.11 PROGRAM COMPONENT INITIATION AND TRANSITION

Program steering committee approval is usually required prior to the initiation of individual components of the program to the extent that the initiation of a component requires: *(a)* the introduction of additional governance structures that are responsible for monitoring and managing the component, and *(b)* the firm commitment of organizational resources for its completion. The program manager frequently acts as the proposer when seeking authorization for the initiation of these components. The approval of the initiation of a new program component generally includes:

- ◆ Developing, modifying, or reconfirming the business case;

- ◆ Ensuring the availability of resources to perform the component;

- ◆ Defining or reconfirming individual accountabilities for management and pursuit of the component;

- ◆ Ensuring the communication of critical component-related information to key stakeholders;

- ◆ Ensuring the establishment of component-specific, program-level quality control plans (when required); and

- ◆ Authorizing the governance structure to track the component's progress against its goals.

The approach used in managing activities within the component is generally dependent on the specific nature of the component. For example, component projects should be managed according to the principles and practices of project management, as defined in the *PMBOK® Guide*, while other programs should be managed according to the principles defined and described in this standard.

Upon initiation of a new component, all program-level documentation and records dealing with the component should be updated to reflect any changes to the affected components.

Approval is generally required for transition and closure of an individual program component. The review of any recommendation for the transition or closure of a program component generally includes:

- ◆ Confirming that the business case for the component has been sufficiently satisfied or that further pursuit of the component's goals should be discontinued,

- ◆ Ensuring appropriate program-level communications of the component's closure to key stakeholders,

- ◆ Ensuring component compliance with program-level quality control plans (when required),

- ◆ Assessing organizational- or program-level lessons learned as a consequence of performance of the component in transition, and

- ◆ Confirming that all other accepted practices for project or program transition or closure have been satisfied.

6.1.12 PROGRAM CLOSURE

The program steering committee reviews and makes decisions on recommendations for the closure of programs. It assesses whether conditions warranting the program are satisfied, and that recommendations for closure of a program are consistent with the current organizational vision, mission, and strategy. Alternatively, programs may be terminated because changes in the organizational strategy or environment have resulted in diminished program benefits or needs. Regardless of the cause for termination, closure procedures should be implemented. Practices and processes commonly used to conduct program closure are described in detail in Section 7.1.4.

At program closure, the importance of effectively transitioning the program governance to operational governance will directly impact the benefits realized (see Section 4.4). The final program report is approved by the governance participants during closure.

6.2 PROGRAM GOVERNANCE ROLES

Establishing an appropriate collaborative relationship between individuals responsible for program governance and program management is critical to the success of programs in delivering the benefits desired by the organization. Program managers rely on the program steering committee (also referred to as the program governance board, oversight committee, or board of directors) members to establish organizational conditions that enable the effective pursuit of programs and to resolve issues that inevitably arise when the needs of their program conflict with the needs of other programs, projects, or ongoing operational activities.

Establishing a collaborative relationship between the program steering committee and program managers is also critical to the success of the organization. In accordance with the program charter, program managers assume responsibility and accountability for effectively managing programs in the pursuit of organizational goals as authorized by the program steering committee.

Program governance structures are best defined in a manner that is specific to the needs of each organization and the requirements of the program. A comprehensive program governance model carefully considers the program and the organizational context in which it is pursued. However, within organizations, the relationship between the program governance and program management functions is often managed by assigning key roles to individuals who are part of those functions and who are recognized as important stakeholders. More details on the factors considered in designing the Program Governance Performance Domain are provided in Section 6.3.

While the design, participants, and roles fulfilling the program governance roles will be specific to the program within an organization, the following roles are commonly used:

◆ **Program sponsor.** An individual or a group that provides resources and support for the program and is accountable for enabling success.

◆ **Program steering committee.** A group of participants representing various program-related interests with the purpose of supporting the program under its authority by providing guidance, endorsements, and approvals through the governance practices. Members are typically executives from organizational groups that support the program's components and operations.

◆ **Program management office (PMO).** A management structure that standardizes the program-related governance processes and facilitates the sharing of resources, methodologies, tools, and techniques.

◆ **Program manager.** The individual within an agency, organization, or corporation who maintains responsibility for the leadership, conduct, and performance of a program. In the context of governance, this role interfaces with the program steering committee and sponsor and manages the program to ensure delivery of the intended benefits.

◆ **Project manager.** The person assigned by the performing organization to lead the team that is responsible for achieving project objectives. In the context of governance, this role interfaces with the program manager and program sponsor and manages the delivery of the project's product, service, or result.

◆ **Other stakeholders.** These stakeholders include the manager of the portfolio of which the program is a component and operational managers receiving the capabilities delivered by the program.

The responsibilities assigned to each of the following roles are for guidance only. Carrying out the activities of the Program Governance Performance Domain will fulfill these responsibilities and the allocation between roles is often dependent on several design factors (see Section 6.3).

6.2.1 PROGRAM SPONSOR

The program sponsor is the individual responsible for committing the application of organizational resources to the program and for program success. The program sponsor role is frequently filled by an executive member of the program steering committee who has a senior role in directing the organization and its investment decisions, and who is personally vested in the success of related organizational programs. In many organizations, the program sponsor acts as the chairperson of the program steering committee and assigns and oversees the progress of the program manager.

Typical responsibilities of the program sponsor are to:

◆ Secure funding for the program and ensure program goals and objectives are aligned with the strategic vision;

◆ Enable the delivery of benefits; and

◆ Remove barriers and obstacles to program success.

As a member or chair of the program steering committee, the sponsor is integral to its responsibilities. It is critical that the organization selects an appropriate program sponsor and then allows him or her to perform the role effectively. Sufficient time and resources should be provided to enable success, which often requires relief from other management and executive duties.

The caliber, experience, and availability of the sponsor impacts the effectiveness of the program and, in some cases, is the difference between perceived success and failure. Very often, the program sponsor is required to drive changes through the organization so that operations can accommodate capabilities delivered by the program, and to secure the available positive benefits and steward the handling of negative benefits. As such, the sponsor is integral to the communication and stakeholder processes. Typically, an effective sponsor exhibits the following attributes:

◆ Ability to influence stakeholders,

◆ Ability to work across different stakeholder groups to find mutually beneficial solutions,

◆ Leadership,

◆ Decision-making authority, and

◆ Effective communication skills.

6.2.2 PROGRAM STEERING COMMITTEE

Most organizations seek to ensure appropriate program governance by establishing program steering committees that are responsible for defining and implementing appropriate governance practices. Program steering committees are usually staffed by individuals who are either individually or collectively recognized as having organizational insight and decision-making authority that is critical to the establishment of program goals, strategy, and operational plans. Program steering committees are usually composed of executive-level stakeholders who have been selected for their strategic insight, technical knowledge, functional responsibilities, operational accountabilities, responsibilities for managing the organization's portfolio, and abilities to represent important stakeholder groups. Often, program steering committees include senior leaders from the functional groups responsible for supporting significant elements of the program, including, for example, the organizational executives and leaders responsible for supporting the program's components. Program steering committees, staffed in this way, improve the likelihood that the activities described in the Program Governance Performance Domain will be well positioned to efficiently address issues or questions that may arise during the performance of the program. Program steering committees ensure that programs are pursued in an environment with appropriate organizational knowledge and expertise, well supported by cohesive policies and processes, and empowered by their access to those with decision-making authority.

Typical responsibilities include:

◆ Provide governance support for the program to include oversight, control, integration, and decision-making functions;

◆ Provide capable governance resources to oversee and monitor program uncertainty and complexity related to achieving benefits delivery;

◆ Ensure program goals and planned benefits align with organizational strategic and operational goals;

◆ Conduct planning sessions to confirm, prioritize, and fund the program;

◆ Endorse or approve program recommendations and changes;

◆ Resolve and remediate escalated program issues and risks;

◆ Provide oversight and monitoring so program benefits are planned, measured, and achieved;

◆ Provide leadership in making, enforcing, carrying out, and communicating decisions;

◆ Define key messages that are to be communicated to stakeholders and ensure they are consistent and transparent;

◆ Review expected benefits and benefits delivery; and

◆ Approve program closure or termination.

In small organizations, a single senior executive may assume the responsibilities of a program oversight committee.

Establishing a single committee that maintains and is accountable for all critical elements of program oversight within an organization is considered to be the most efficient means for providing effective and adaptive governance oversight. However, under certain circumstances, some programs may need to report to multiple steering committees; for example, programs that are sponsored and overseen jointly by private and governmental organizations, programs managed as collaborations between private but otherwise competitive organizations, or programs in exceedingly complex environments whose subject matter experts cannot be effectively assembled into a single program steering committee. Under these circumstances, it is critical that the systems and methods for program governance and the authority for program decision making be clearly established in the program governance plan.

6.2.3 THE PROGRAM MANAGEMENT OFFICE

The program management office (PMO) facilitates the governance practices. It is a management structure that standardizes the program-related governance processes and facilitates the sharing of resources, methodologies, tools, and techniques. It provides professional expertise using staff highly trained in applying program governance practices to provide oversight, support, and decision-making capability to the program. The PMO role may extend to monitoring compliance to program management practices.

The design and formation of a PMO is tailored to its environment. For example, organizations pursuing exceptionally large, complicated, or complex programs may establish multiple PMOs, each of which may be dedicated solely to the conduct of one or more critical organizational programs.

Alternatively, organizations pursuing multiple programs often seek to ensure a high level of consistency and professionalism in the management and governance of their programs by creating a PMO as a formal center of excellence in program governance practices that services a portfolio of different programs. For any program, the PMO may be created or may leverage an existing function. Depending on the context of the program, individuals with specific skills, such as change and benefits management specialists can be allocated to the PMO.

On occasion, the functions of a PMO may be delegated to an individual manager with an exceptional understanding of program management and governance practices, or directly to the individual program managers responsible for oversight of the organization's programs. See Section 1.9 for more information on the PMO.

6.2.4 PROGRAM MANAGER

The program manager is the individual responsible for management and oversight of the program's interactions with the program governance function.

The program manager is granted authority to make decisions on behalf of the program steering committee. For decisions outside of this agreed-upon authority, it is necessary for the program manager to secure authorization from the program steering committee. A number of factors may influence the authority granted to the program team, including the experience of the program manager, the size and complexity of the program and its components, and the degree of coordination required to manage the program within the context of the larger organization.

The program manager ensures that the program goals and objectives remain aligned with the overall strategic objectives of the organization. Typical governance-related responsibilities include:

◆ Assess the governance framework, including organizational structure, policies, and procedures, and, in some cases, establish the program governance framework;

◆ Oversee program conformance to governance policies and processes;

◆ Manage program interactions with the steering committee and sponsor;

◆ Manage interdependencies between components within the program;

◆ Monitor and manage program risks, performance, and communications;

◆ Manage program risks and issues and escalate critical risks and issues beyond the program manager's control to the steering committee;

◆ Monitor and report on overall program funding and health;

◆ Assess program outcomes and request authorization from the steering committee to change overall program strategies;

◆ Create, monitor, and communicate the program integrated roadmap and key internal and external dependencies; and

◆ Manage, monitor, and track overall program benefits realization.

Program goals are pursued and benefits are delivered by means of the authorization and initiation of components. The authorization of components under the direction of a parent program is conceptually the same as the authorization of the parent program itself by its program steering committee. Thus, programs have a function similar to that of a governance board. Program managers and program teams may become responsible for a governance function that is often referred to as component governance. In this role, program managers are responsible for defining the framework, functions, and processes by which their program's components will be monitored and managed. The degree of autonomy granted to program managers for oversight of their components, and the mechanisms provided by parent programs, differs among organizations and (at times) among programs being managed within a single organization. While some organizations choose to have components governed by the same program governance structure described for a parent program, others allow the parent program to assume independent responsibility for governance of program components. Under such circumstances, a program manager may assume responsibility for establishing a governing framework to manage components within the parent program.

See Section 1.7 for more information on the role of the program manager.

6.2.5 PROJECT MANAGER(S)

In the context of a program, the project manager role generally refers to an individual responsible for oversight or management of a project that is being pursued as a component of the program. In this context, the project manager responsibilities are defined in the *PMBOK® Guide*. They include effective planning, performing, and tracking of a program's component project(s), and delivery of the project's outputs as defined in the project's charter and in the program management plan. In this capacity, the project manager is subject to component governance oversight by the program manager (acting in a role analogous to that of the program steering committee) and to the program team. While the role is not always central to program governance, the typical governance-related responsibilities of a project manager include:

- Manage project interactions with the program manager, steering committee, and sponsor;
- Oversee project conformance to governance policies and processes;
- Monitor and manage performance and communications;
- Manage project risks and issues and escalate critical risks and issues beyond the project manager's control to the program manager, sponsor, or steering committee of the project;
- Manage internal and external dependencies for the project; and
- Foster engagement of key stakeholders.

6.2.6 OTHER STAKEHOLDERS

Several other stakeholders may have program governance related roles. The portfolio manager may have a role in ensuring that a program is selected, prioritized, and staffed according to the organization's plan for realizing desired benefits.

As the program progresses, representatives of the business, such as functional representatives and product owners ensure that the program's direction is aligned to the end customers' potentially evolving requirements.

When the program delivers a capability to the organization, the expected or potential benefits can only be realized when the organization is prepared to integrate the capability into its operations. The operational manager is generally responsible for receiving and integrating the capabilities delivered by other program components for achieving desired organizational benefits. This integration initially often leads to disruption and, over the longer term, a steady state that is different from the previous environment. It is therefore important to the success of the organization and program that the capability is integrated effectively. The operational manager is supported by individual(s) assigned the role to manage this change. Such individuals can be the sponsor, representative(s) from the receiving business area, program manager, project manager, and in many cases a specialist in managing business change. This role has governance implications as it informs and performs the governance practices described in Section 6.1. Typically, the individual in this role will be supported by a team from the corresponding business area.

Other governance-associated roles include specialists in certain aspects of the domain, including risk specialists, buyers, and contracting experts to develop and govern agreements with third-party vendors.

6.3 PROGRAM GOVERNANCE DESIGN AND IMPLEMENTATION

Program governance begins with the identification of governance participants and the establishment of governance practices. There is also a need to define the specific expectations for how governance-related roles are filled and responsibilities discharged. Governance practices may differ depending on the sector or industry that the organization serves. Governance of programs in such diverse fields as national or local government, aerospace and defense, banking and financing, and pharmaceutical development may have remarkably different needs based on the unique political, regulatory, legal, technical, and competitive environments in which they operate. In each case, however, a sponsor organization seeks to implement governance practices that enable the organization to monitor the program's support of the organizational strategy.

Effective governance ensures that strategic alignment is optimized and that the program's targeted benefits are delivered as expected. Governance participants also confirm that all stakeholders are appropriately engaged and that appropriate supportive tools and processes are defined and effectively leveraged. Governance practices provide the foundation for ensuring that decisions are made rationally and with appropriate justification, and that the responsibilities and accountabilities are clearly defined and applied. All of these activities are accomplished within the policies and standards of the host and partner organizations and are measured to attain compliance.

The design of program governance can have a significant influence on the success of the program. In extreme cases, inappropriate governance may create more problems than its absence as it can engender a false sense of alignment, progress, and success. There are many factors to consider when designing the program governance rules and framework. Common factors to consider when optimizing and tailoring program governance include:

◆ **Legislative environment.** Programs that are significantly influenced by changing legislation may benefit from governance designed for direct interaction with the legislative authorities. In other cases, the interaction is performed by elements of corporate governance on behalf of the program.

◆ **Decision-making hierarchy.** It is critical for decision-making responsibility to be at the level where competence, accountability, and authority reside. There are complexities to this approach. For example, in organizations where employees are not ultimately accountable for their actions or not made to feel accountable for their actions, there is a greater need for controlling practices. In other circumstances, a highly regarded, successful, and experienced program manager and team may be given greater autonomy and decision-making powers than is typically given to program managers.

◆ **Optimized governance.** Generally it makes sense for the size of the program governance to be optimized and to be as streamlined as possible, while still able to perform the practices of the domain. This will lead to role clarity, effective and targeted support from the organization, and ultimately more rapid and effective decision making, endorsements, and approvals. Program governance should not duplicate program management activity.

◆ **Alignment with portfolio and organizational governance.** Program governance is impacted by the portfolio governance that it supports. The degree to which program governance should align with organizational governance is based on the number, type, and relative importance of the program governance's interactions with corporate groups and governance. Typically, the need for alignment with organizational governance is greatest in the program definition stage as the program governance and the program itself are being formulated.

◆ **Program delivery.** A program that regularly delivers benefits to the organization is likely to require different governance than a program delivering all or most of the benefits at the end. Regular delivery of benefits potentially requires constant change in the operations of the organization and the governance to manage this change is critical throughout the life cycle.

◆ **Contracting.** A program being managed and staffed by employees of the receiving organization is likely to require a different level of governance than a program being delivered by an external party when, in such cases, the management of the legal agreement requires a different governance focus.

◆ **Risk of failure.** The greater the perceived risk of program failure, the greater the likelihood the governance team will monitor progress and success more diligently. This may manifest in a higher frequency of health checks and less decision-making delegation to the program team.

◆ **Strategic importance.** High-value programs critical to the success of the organization and delivering benefits that need to be completely aligned with the strategy may require different or more senior participants on the governance team.

◆ **Program management office (PMO).** In many project- or program-based organizations, a centralized PMO supports the governance of all programs for that organization. In other organizations, PMOs may be formed specifically for a given program.

◆ **Program funding structure.** When funding is secured from outside the delivery organization, for example from the World Bank, there are likely implications on the design of the governance and the skills required.

In addition to these factors, the phase of the life cycle also influences program governance, because the relative importance of different governance practices differs as the program progresses. The corresponding design of the governance should align with required practices in a timely manner.

As a result of the factors described in Section 6.3, there are many considerations to account for in the optimization of program governance. Once program governance is designed and implemented, it is important to exercise mechanisms to assess its effectiveness and to continually improve and optimize it.

For a broader discussion of program governance within the context of organizational, portfolio, and project governance, see *Governance of Portfolios, Programs, and Projects: A Practice Guide* [7].

7

PROGRAM LIFE CYCLE MANAGEMENT

Program Life Cycle Management is the performance domain that manages program activities required to facilitate effective program definition, program delivery, and program closure.

This section includes:

7.1 The Program Life Cycle

7.2 Program Activities and Integration Management

In order to ensure the realization of benefits, programs provide the necessary alignment of the organization's strategic goals and objectives with the individual components. These components may include projects, subsidiary programs, and additional program-related activities that are necessary to achieve the specified goals and objectives. Since programs, by nature, involve a certain level of uncertainty, change, complexity, and interdependency among the various components, it is useful to establish a common and consistent set of processes that can be applied across phases. These discrete phases, which may sometimes overlap, constitute the program life cycle. Program Life Cycle Management spans the duration of the program, during which it contributes to and integrates with the other program domains as well as the supporting program activities.

7.1 THE PROGRAM LIFE CYCLE

Programs function similarly to projects in that the program is defined, benefits are delivered, and the program is closed. However, unlike projects, programs involve the coordination and sequencing of multiple components above what is required at an individual project level. The activities executed within the program life cycle are dependent on the specific type of program and typically begin before funding is approved or when the program manager is assigned. There is often considerable effort expended prior to defining and approving a program. See Sections 3 and 6 for more information on Program Strategy Alignment and Program Governance.

During program delivery, components are authorized, planned, and executed, and benefits are delivered. Program closure is then approved by the program steering committee when the desired benefits or program objectives have been realized or the steering committee has determined that the program should be terminated. Reasons for early termination may be a change in organizational strategy with which the program is no longer aligned or an assessment that the planned benefits may no longer be achievable.

7.1.1 PROGRAM LIFE CYCLE PHASES OVERVIEW

Programs often span long durations—multiple years and, in some cases, decades. Regardless of duration, all programs follow a similar trajectory.

To successfully deliver benefits to an organization, programs are implemented using three major phases, which include:

◆ **Program Definition Phase.** This phase consists of program activities conducted to authorize the program and develop the program roadmap required to achieve the expected results. As part of program definition, the program business case and program charter are formulated. Once approved, the program management plan is prepared.

◆ **Program Delivery Phase.** Program delivery comprises the program activities performed to produce the intended results of each component in accordance with the program management plan. Throughout this phase, individual components are initiated, planned, executed, transitioned, and closed, while benefits are delivered, transitioned, and sustained.

◆ **Program Closure Phase.** This phase includes the program activities necessary to transition the program benefits to the sustaining organization and formally close the program in a controlled manner. During program closure, the program is transitioned and closed or terminated early, or work is transitioned to another program.

Figure 7-1 shows the phases that compose the program life cycle. These phases are further explained in Sections 7.1.2 through 7.1.4.

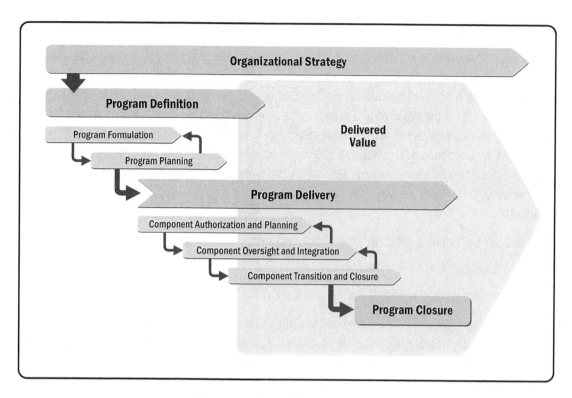

Figure 7-1. Program Life Cycle Phases

7.1.2 PROGRAM DEFINITION PHASE

The program definition phase includes program activities conducted to authorize the program and develop the program roadmap required to achieve the expected results; it typically includes activities that are performed as the result of an organization's plan to fulfill strategic objectives or achieve a desired state within an organization's portfolio. There may be a number of activities executed by a portfolio management body prior to the start of the program definition phase. The portfolio management activity develops concepts (for products, services, or organizational outcomes), scope frameworks, initial requirements, timelines, deliverables, and acceptable cost guidelines.

The primary purpose of the program definition phase is to progressively elaborate the goals and objectives to be addressed by the program, define the expected program outcomes and benefits, and seek approval for the program. Program definition generally falls into two distinct but overlapping subphases: program formulation and program planning. The program manager is selected and assigned during program formulation.

7.1.2.1 PROGRAM FORMULATION

Program formulation involves the development of the program business case which states the overall expected benefits to be addressed by the program in support of the strategic initiatives. During this subphase, the sponsoring organization also assigns a program sponsor to oversee and govern the program. The sponsor's key responsibilities include securing financing for the program and selecting the program manager who is responsible for conducting and managing the program. The assignment of the program manager and the definition of his or her roles, responsibilities, and organizational interfaces should be performed as early as possible, as this individual effectively guides the program formulation activity and facilitates the development of the required outputs. To demonstrate how the program will deliver the desired organizational benefits, the sponsor, sponsoring organization, and the program manager work closely together to:

◆ Initiate studies and estimates of scope, resources, and cost;

◆ Develop an initial risk assessment; and

◆ Develop a program charter and roadmap.

Studies of scope, resources, and cost are also performed to assess the organization's ability to deliver the program. At this time, the candidate program is compared with other organizational initiatives to determine the priority of the program under consideration. This information serves as critical input into the creation of the business case, if it was not developed by the portfolio management function. When the business case was developed prior to program formulation, it is revised and updated accordingly. Additionally, an initial risk assessment is conducted to analyze threats and opportunities. This analysis helps determine the probability of the program's successful delivery of organizational benefits and helps identify risk response strategies and plans. See Section 8 for additional information on program risks.

The program charter serves as the primary document that is reviewed by the program steering committee to decide if the program will be authorized. Approval of the charter formally authorizes the commencement of the program, provides the program manager with the authority to apply organizational resources to program activities, and connects the program to the organization's ongoing work and strategic priorities. If the program is not authorized, this information should be recorded and captured in a lessons learned repository.

The contents of the program charter generally consist of the following questions and their answers:

◆ **Justification.** Why is the program important and what does it achieve?

◆ **Vision.** What is the end state and how will it benefit the organization?

◆ **Strategic alignment.** What are the key strategic drivers and the program's relationship to the organizational strategic objectives and any other ongoing strategic initiatives? (See Section 3 for more information on Program Strategy Alignment.)

◆ **Benefits.** What are the key outcomes required to achieve the program vision and benefits?

◆ **Scope.** What is included within the program and what is considered to be out of scope at a high level?

◆ **Benefit strategy.** What is the approach to ensure the realization of the planned benefits? (See Section 4 for more information on Program Benefits Management.)

◆ **Assumptions and constraints.** What are the assumptions, constraints, dependencies, and external factors considered and how have they shaped or limited the program's objectives?

◆ **Components.** How are the projects and other program components configured to deliver the program and the intended benefits?

◆ **Risks and issues.** What are the initial risks and issues identified during the preparation of the program roadmap?

◆ **Timeline.** What is the total length of the program, including all key milestone dates?

◆ **Resources needed.** What are the estimated program costs and resource needs (i.e., staff, training, travel, etc.)?

◆ **Stakeholder considerations.** Who are the key stakeholders, who are the most important stakeholders, and what is the initial strategy to engage them? This information contributes to the development of the communications management plan. (See Section 5 for more information on Program Stakeholder Engagement.)

◆ **Program governance.** What is the recommended governance structure to manage, control, and support the program? What are the recommended governance structures to guide and oversee the program components, including reporting requirements? What authority does the program manager possess? This information is updated in the program governance plan. (See Section 6 for more information on Program Governance.)

The outputs of program formulation may continue to be updated throughout the program definition phase as business results are measured and the planned outcomes become more defined.

7.1.2.2 PROGRAM PLANNING

Program planning commences upon formal approval of the program charter by the program steering committee. In this phase, a governance structure is established, the initial program organization is defined, and a team is assembled to develop the program management plan. The program management plan is the document that integrates the program's subsidiary plans and establishes the management controls and overall plan for integrating and managing the program's individual components. These controls measure performance against the program management plan using information that is collected and consolidated from the constituent projects. Its main purpose is to ensure the program is continually aligned with the strategic priorities of the organization in order to deliver the expected benefits. The program management plan is developed based on the organization's strategic plan, business case, program charter, roadmap, and any other outputs from program formulation.

This plan is the key output created during program planning and may be combined into one plan or multiple plans that include the following subsidiary documents:

◆ Benefits management plan (see Section 4.2.1),

◆ Stakeholder engagement plan (see Section 5.3),

◆ Governance plan (see Section 6.1.1),

◆ Change management plan (see Section 8.1.2.1),

◆ Communications management plan (see Section 8.1.2.2),

◆ Financial management plan (see Section 8.1.2.5),

◆ Information management plan (see Section 8.1.2.6),

◆ Procurement management plan (see Section 8.1.2.7),

◆ Quality management plan (see Section 8.1.2.8),

◆ Resource management plan (see Section 8.1.2.9),

◆ Risk management plan (see Section 8.1.2.10),

◆ Schedule management plan (see Section 8.1.2.11),

◆ Scope management plan (see Section 8.1.2.12), and

◆ Program roadmap (see Section 3.3).

Once the program management plan has been approved, the program delivery phase can begin. However, it is important to remember that development of this plan is an iterative activity since it is prepared early in the program life cycle and conflicting priorities, assumptions, and constraints may arise due to changes in critical factors, such as business goals, deliverables, benefits, time, and cost. To address these factors, updates and revisions to the program management plan and its subsidiary plans are approved or rejected through the Program Governance Performance Domain.

The program delivery phase begins after the program management plan is reviewed and formally approved. Programs are typically authorized by a program steering committee.

7.1.3 PROGRAM DELIVERY PHASE

The program delivery phase includes program activities performed to produce the intended results of each component in accordance with the program management plan. This phase is considered iterative instead of linear, as the capabilities produced by each component are integrated into the overall program to facilitate delivery of the intended program benefits. The program management team provides oversight and support to position the components for successful completion. The component work and activities are integrated under the program umbrella to facilitate the management and delivery of program benefits. The work in this phase includes the program and execution of the program components. Component management plans (covering cost management, scope management, schedule management, risk management, resource management, etc.) are developed at the component level (component-level work) and integrated at the program level (integrative work) to maintain alignment with the program direction to deliver the program benefits. Interactions with components to accomplish goals, manage changes, and mitigate risks and issues are managed through the program in order to position the program for success.

Programs often have a significant level of uncertainty. While the program management plan and program roadmap may document the intended direction and benefits of the program, the full suite of program components may not be known in the program definition phase. To accommodate this uncertainty, the program manager needs to continually oversee the components throughout this phase and, when necessary, replan for their proper integration or realign to accommodate changes in program direction through adaptive change. The program manager is also responsible for managing this group of components in a consistent and coordinated way in order to achieve results that could not be obtained by managing the components as stand-alone efforts. Each program component will progress through the following program delivery subphases:

◆ Component authorization and planning,

◆ Component oversight and integration, and

◆ Component transition and closure.

Program delivery ends when program governance determines that the specific criteria for this phase have been satisfied or a decision is made to terminate the program.

7.1.3.1 COMPONENT AUTHORIZATION AND PLANNING

Component authorization involves the initiation of components based on the organization's specified criteria and individual business cases developed for each component. These criteria are generally included in the program governance plan. The Program Governance Performance Domain provides guidance for processes leading to component authorization. A number of activities are required to verify that a component properly supports the program's outcomes and aligns with the strategy and ongoing work of the organization prior to authorization. These activities may include performing a needs analysis, conducting a feasibility study, or creating a plan to ensure the projects realize their intended benefits. See Section 6 for more information on Program Governance.

Component planning is performed throughout the duration of the program delivery phase in response to events that require significant replanning or new component initiation requests (submitted by the requesting component). Component planning includes the activities needed to integrate the component into the program to position each component for successful execution. These activities involve formalizing the scope of the work to be accomplished by the component and identifying the deliverables that will satisfy the program's goals and benefits.

Each component has associated management plans. These may include a project management plan, transition plan, operations plan, maintenance plan, or other type of plan depending upon the type of work under consideration. The appropriate information from each component plan is integrated into the associated program management plan. This includes information used by the program to help manage and oversee the overall program's progress.

7.1.3.2 COMPONENT OVERSIGHT AND INTEGRATION

In the context of a program, some components may produce benefits as individual components, while other components are integrated with others before the associated benefits may be realized. Each component team executes its associated plans and program integrative work. Throughout this activity, components provide status and other information to the program manager and to their associated components so their efforts may be integrated into and coordinated with the overall program activities. There may be cases where the program manager may initiate a new component to consolidate the integration efforts of multiple components. Without this step, individual components may produce deliverables; however, the benefits may not be realized without the coordinated delivery.

7.1.3.3 COMPONENT TRANSITION AND CLOSURE

After the program components have produced deliverables and coordinated the successful delivery of their products, services, or results, these components are typically scheduled for closure or transition to operations or ongoing work. Component transition addresses the need for ongoing activities such as product support, service management, change management, user engagement, or customer support from a program component to an operational support function in order for the ongoing benefits to be achieved. The criteria for performing these activities and the organizational expectations are documented in the governance plan.

Prior to the end of the program delivery phase, all component areas are reviewed to verify that the benefits were delivered and to transition any remaining projects and sustaining activities. The final status is reviewed with the program sponsor and program steering committee before the authorizing formal program closure.

7.1.4 PROGRAM CLOSURE PHASE

The program closure phase includes program activities necessary to transition program benefits to the sustaining organization and formally close the program in a controlled manner. During program transition, the program steering committee is consulted to determine whether: *(a)* the program has met all of the desired benefits and that all transition work has been performed within the component transition, or *(b)* there is another program or sustaining activity that will oversee the ongoing benefits for which this program was chartered. In the second instance, there may be work required to transition the resources, responsibilities, knowledge, and lessons learned to another sustaining entity. Once the transitioning activities are completed, the program manager receives approval from the sponsoring organization to formally close the program. During this closure phase, specific activities are performed, which are described in detail in Section 7.2.2.5.

7.2 PROGRAM ACTIVITIES AND INTEGRATION MANAGEMENT

As defined in Section 1, program management refers to the alignment of various components, such as projects and other programs, to achieve the planned program goals. The practices applied during this process are used to optimize or integrate the costs, schedules, and effort of the individual components to gain control and deliver maximum benefits at the program level instead of the component level.

Program activities and integration management are concerned with collectively utilizing the resources, knowledge, and skills available to effectively deploy multiple components throughout the program life cycle. This process also involves making decisions regarding:

◆ Competing demands and priorities,

◆ Risks,

◆ Resource allocations,

◆ Changes due to uncertainty and complexity of the program scope,

◆ Interdependencies among components, and

◆ Coordination of work to meet the program objectives.

Program activities and integration management are more cyclical and iterative in nature as adjustments may be required based on the actual outcomes and benefits produced to realign the program with the strategic priorities.

7.2.1 PROGRAM ACTIVITIES OVERVIEW

All work performed in a program for the purpose of overall program management is collectively known as program activities. Typically, program activities are interdependent and complementary since the deliverables produced from one particular activity may be necessary to perform another activity. The names and descriptions of these activities may appear to be similar to those of project activities or processes; however, their content, scope, and complexity are different. For example, project risk management activities focus on risks to project execution and success, while program risk management incorporates escalated project risks and program risks and also monitors interdependencies that affect multiple component projects.

The processes and tools used in project-level activities can be found in the latest edition of the *PMBOK® Guide*. The corresponding program activities encompass a greater number of inputs and typically broader scope. For example, results of the individual component project risk planning efforts provide input to the program risk planning effort. Risk control is performed continuously at both the component level and the program level itself; project-level risks may be escalated to the program level or may have a cumulative effect that requires the risks to be addressed at the program level.

It is important to note that program activities directly support the individual components to ensure the component activities help achieve the program objectives. The deliverables created at the project level that directly contribute to the program benefits and milestones achieved are monitored at the program level by the program manager to ensure consistency with the overall program strategy. Management of component-level activities is still handled by the project manager.

7.2.2 PROGRAM INTEGRATION MANAGEMENT

Program integration management is the core activity that occurs across the entire program life cycle. It includes the activities needed to identify, define, combine, unify, and coordinate multiple components into the program. Throughout the program integration activities, there are numerous interactions with other program performance domains (see Section 2). This section focuses on the following activities and when they are performed throughout the program life cycle phases:

◆ Program infrastructure development (see Section 7.2.2.1),

◆ Program delivery management (see Section 7.2.2.2),

◆ Program performance monitoring and controlling (see Section 7.2.2.3),

◆ Benefits sustainment and program transition (see Section 7.2.2.4), and

◆ Program closeout (see Section 7.2.2.5).

7.2.2.1 PROGRAM INFRASTRUCTURE DEVELOPMENT

Program infrastructure development is performed to investigate, assess, and plan the support structure that will assist the program in achieving its goals. This activity is initiated in the program definition phase and may be repeated again at any time during the program life cycle in order to update or modify the infrastructure.

The primary purpose of program infrastructure development is twofold. It establishes both the management and technical resources of the program and its components. This infrastructure refers to both personnel and to program-specific tools, facilities, and finances used to manage the program.

Although the program manager is assigned during program definition, the program management core team is designated as part of establishing the program infrastructure. The core team members may not necessarily be assigned full-time to the program; however, these key stakeholders are instrumental in determining and developing the program's infrastructure requirements.

For many programs, the program management office (PMO) is a core part of the program infrastructure. It supports the management and coordination of the program and component work. The PMO also establishes consistent policy, standards, and training for programs in the organization. Another key element of the program infrastructure is the program management information system (PMIS). A PMIS consists of tools used to collect, integrate, and communicate information critical to the effective management of one or more organizational programs. An effective PMIS incorporates the following:

◆ Software tools;

◆ Documents, data, and knowledge repositories;

◆ Configuration management tools;

◆ Change management system;

◆ Risk database and analysis tools;

◆ Financial management systems;

◆ Earned value management activities and tools;

◆ Requirements management activities and tools; and

◆ Other tools and activities as required.

These resources are separate and distinct from the resources required to manage the individual components within the program. The distinguishing factor is that the majority of resources and program costs are managed at the component level instead of the program level.

7.2.2.2 PROGRAM DELIVERY MANAGEMENT

Program delivery management includes the management, oversight, integration, and optimization of the program components that will deliver the capabilities and benefits required for the organization to realize value. These activities are performed throughout the program delivery phase and relate to the initiation, change, transition, and closure of program components.

It is typically the role of the program manager to present a request to initiate a new component or project. This request is evaluated by the program steering committee against the organization's approved selection criteria. A decision is made utilizing the governance function on whether the component should be initiated. If the component is approved, the program manager may need to redefine the priorities of existing program components to ensure optimal resource allocation and management of interdependencies. Component initiation may be delayed or accelerated as defined by the program team and its needs. During the course of program delivery, change requests that fall within the program manager's authority level will be approved or rejected to manage performance and any changes to the program management plan.

As the program components reach the end of their respective life cycles or as planned program-level milestones are achieved, the program manager collaborates with the customer or sponsor to present a request to close or transition the component. This formal request is sent to the program steering committee for review and approval. The process of component transition includes making updates to the program roadmap. These updates reflect both go/no-go decisions and approved change requests that affect the high-level milestones, scope, or timing of major stages scheduled throughout the program.

7.2.2.3 PROGRAM PERFORMANCE MONITORING AND CONTROLLING

Monitoring and controlling activities are performed by both program- and project-level components during delivery management. These activities include collecting, measuring, and disseminating performance information to track progress against the program objectives and assess overall program trends. Continuous monitoring gives the program management team insight into the current health of the program and identifies areas that require special attention. Monitoring activities determine if and when controlling activities, such as corrective or preventive action, are needed to bring the program back in alignment with the strategic priorities.

Based on thresholds authorized by program governance, requests to execute corrective or preventive action, in addition to adaptive change, may be approved at the component or program level. When the requests exceed the established program-level thresholds, the requests are presented to the program steering committee for approval. Typical outputs of this ongoing activity include program performance reports and forecasts.

Program performance reports include a summary of the progress of all program components. They describe whether the program's goals will be met and benefits will be successfully delivered according to plan. These reports generally provide current status information about what work has been accomplished (especially milestones and phase gates); what work remains to be completed; earned value; and risks, issues, and changes under consideration. Forecasts enable the program manager and other key stakeholders to assess the likelihood of achieving planned outcomes and to provide predictions of the program's future state based on the current information and knowledge available.

7.2.2.4 BENEFITS SUSTAINMENT AND PROGRAM TRANSITION

Some program components produce immediate benefits while others require a handoff or transition to another organization in order for the ongoing benefit to be realized. Benefits sustainment may be achieved through operations, maintenance, new projects, or other initiatives and efforts. This activity transcends the scope of individual program components since this work is typically performed as the program is closed. During this subphase, the stewardship of sustaining the benefits may need to transition to another organization, entity, or subsequent program.

7.2.2.5 PROGRAM CLOSEOUT

A program is closed either because the program charter is fulfilled or internal/external conditions arise that bring the program to an early end. These conditions may include changes in the business case that no longer make the program necessary or a determination that the expected benefits cannot be achieved. During closeout, benefits may have been fully realized or they may continue to be realized and managed as part of organizational operations. Successful completion of the program is judged against the approved business case, actual program outcomes, and the current goals and strategic objectives of the organization. All components should be completed or canceled and all contracts should be formally closed before the program itself is closed. Once these criteria have been met, the program will receive formal closure acceptance from the program steering committee.

As part of the program governance plan, a final program report may be required to document critical information that can be applied to improve the success of future programs and component projects. This final report may consist of:

◆ Financial and performance assessments,

◆ Lessons learned,

◆ Successes and failures,

◆ Identified areas for improvement,

◆ Risk management outcomes,

◆ Unforeseen risks,

◆ Customer sign-off,

◆ Reason(s) for program closeout,

◆ History of all baselines, and

◆ Archive plan for program documentation.

Upon program completion, knowledge transfer is performed when the program management team assesses the program's performance and shares lessons learned with the organization. The final program report may also be updated with this information. Lessons learned should be readily accessible to any existing or future program to facilitate continuous learning and avoid similar pitfalls encountered in other programs. This knowledge transfer also supplements benefits sustainment by providing the new supporting organization with any relevant documentation, training, or materials (see Sections 3.4.2.5 and 8.2.4.1 for more information).

It is important to ensure that program resources are appropriately released as the program is being closed. This may involve the reallocation or reassignment of team members and funding to other initiatives or programs. Reassignment of resources at the component level could include transitioning resources to another component already in execution or another program within the organization that requires a similar skill set. Refer to the *PMBOK® Guide* for more information regarding resource disposition for component projects.

7.2.3 MAPPING OF THE PROGRAM LIFE CYCLE TO PROGRAM ACTIVITIES

Table 7-1 maps the program management life cycle's three major phases to the program supporting activities discussed in Section 8. Although these supporting activities occur throughout the program life cycle, each activity is mapped where most of the work takes place. Informal preplanning exercises may take place in earlier phases for each consideration.

Table 7-1. Mapping of Program Management Life Cycle Phases to Supporting Activities

Supporting Program Activities	Program Life Cycle Phases		
	Program Definition	Program Delivery	Program Closure
Program Change Management	Program Change Assessment Program Change Management Planning	Program Change Monitoring and Controlling	
Program Communications Management	Program Communications Assessment Program Communications Management Planning	Program Information Distribution Program Reporting	
Program Financial Management	Program Initial Cost Estimation Program Cost Estimation Program Financial Framework Establishment Program Financial Management Planning	Program Cost Budgeting Component Cost Estimation Program Financial Monitoring and Controlling	Program Financial Closure
Program Information Management	Program Information Management Planning	Lessons Learned	Program Information Archiving and Transition
Program Procurement Management	Program Procurement Assessment Program Procurement Management Planning	Program Contract Administration	Program Procurement Closure
Program Quality Management	Program Quality Assessment Program Quality Management Planning	Program Quality Control	
Program Resource Management	Program Resource Requirements Estimation Program Resource Management Planning	Resource Interdependency Management	Program Resource Transition
Program Risk Management	Program Initial Risk Assessment Program Risk Management Planning	Program Risk Monitoring and Controlling Program Risk Identification Program Risk Analysis Program Risk Response Management	Program Risk Transition
Program Schedule Management	Program Schedule Assessment Program Schedule Management Planning	Program Schedule Monitoring and Controlling	
Program Scope Management	Program Scope Assessment Program Scope Management Planning	Program Scope Monitoring and Controlling	

8

PROGRAM ACTIVITIES

Program activities are tasks and work conducted to support a program and which contribute throughout the program life cycle.

This section includes:

8.1 Program Definition Phase Activities

8.2 Program Delivery Phase Activities

8.3 Program Closure Phase Activities

Given the scope and complexity of a program, numerous supporting program activities are performed throughout the program life cycle. The definitions and terminology associated with these activities at the program level are very similar to those at the project level. However, program activities operate at a higher level, dealing with multiple projects and other programs, and addressing links between the program and the organizational strategy. While they may utilize component-level information, the activities generally integrate the information to reflect a program perspective.

The program activities that support program management and governance include:

◆ Program Change Management,

◆ Program Communications Management,

◆ Program Financial Management,

◆ Program Information Management,

◆ Program Procurement Management,

◆ Program Quality Management,

◆ Program Resource Management,

◆ Program Risk Management,

◆ Program Schedule Management, and

◆ Program Scope Management.

The program activities enable a strategic approach to planning, monitoring and controlling, and delivering program outputs and benefits. Program management supporting activities require coordination with functional groups in the organization—but in a broader context than similar activities supporting a single project.

8.1 PROGRAM DEFINITION PHASE ACTIVITIES

The program definition phase establishes and confirms the business case for the program and then develops the detailed plan for its delivery. This phase is divided into two parts: program formulation and program planning.

8.1.1 PROGRAM FORMULATION ACTIVITIES

In program formulation, the high-level scope, risks, costs, and expected benefits of the program are assessed to confirm that the program represents a viable way forward for the organization and is well aligned with the organization's strategic objectives. Program activities supporting program formulation are often exploratory in nature, looking at a number of possible alternatives to ensure the one best aligned with strategy and organizational preferences can be identified and approved for inclusion into the program. However, in some cases, program formulation leads to the conclusion that the program does not have a strong business case and the program is stopped.

Figure 8-1 illustrates how program formulation activities contribute to the development of the program business case and program charter through the core activity of program integration management (see Section 7.2.2).

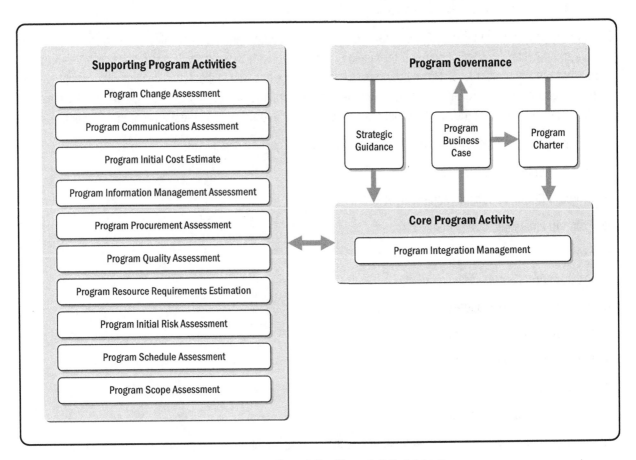

Figure 8-1. Program Formulation Phase Activity Interaction

8.1.1.1 PROGRAM CHANGE ASSESSMENT

As part of program formulation, potential change management considerations are identified and assessed to help develop the program's business case. The program change assessment identifies sources of change, such as the volatility of the enterprise environmental factors, the sensitivity of the proposed program's business case to changes in organizational strategy, and the possible frequency and magnitude of changes that may arise from components during program delivery. It then estimates the likelihood and possible impacts of the changes that could arise from these sources and proposes measures that could be taken to enable the program to respond to such changes in a positive, rather than disruptive, way.

The output of this activity is the program change assessment, which is an input to the program business case, program charter, and program change management planning.

8.1.1.2 PROGRAM COMMUNICATIONS ASSESSMENT

Program Communications Management is different from project communications. Since it affects a wider array of stakeholders with widely varying communication needs, different communication approaches and methods of delivery are required.

An initial assessment of the communication needs of the program is a key input to the program charter. Given the broad scope of a program, a wide range of stakeholders may be involved, and maintaining effective communications with internal and external stakeholders can prevent more serious problems from arising. It may be useful as part of program formulation to survey program stakeholders to identify their expectations for its outcome and their interests in staying informed and involved during its delivery.

The output of this activity is the program communications assessment, which is an input to the stakeholder engagement plan and program communications management planning.

8.1.1.3 PROGRAM INITIAL COST ESTIMATION

A critical element of the program's business case is an estimate of its overall cost and an assessment of the level of confidence in this estimate. An initial cost estimate is prepared in the program definition phase to determine the cost of its planning and delivery. This initial rough order-of-magnitude estimate allows financial decision makers to decide if the program should be funded. Because of the limited information, time, and resources available, it may be difficult to develop a highly detailed or accurate cost estimate. Often the numbers will only be accurate to a rough order of magnitude. Given these challenges, it can also be useful to identify the nature and sources of those costs that could not be estimated.

The output of this activity is the program initial cost estimate, which is an input to the program business case and the program charter and detailed program cost estimation during program planning.

8.1.1.4 PROGRAM INFORMATION MANAGEMENT ASSESSMENT

A program will likely generate a large amount of documentation, data, and other records throughout its life cycle. How easily this information can be collected, shared, and maintained may have a significant effect on both program team efficiency and how the program is perceived by its stakeholders. The information management needs of the program should be considered as part of program formulation so that possible financial, organizational, or resource implications can be assessed.

The output of this activity is the program information management assessment, which is an input to the program business case, program charter, and program information management planning during program planning.

8.1.1.5 PROGRAM PROCUREMENT ASSESSMENT

An assessment of the procurement needs of a program can be a valuable input to the program charter. Although procurement policies and practices are typically part of the organizational or environmental factors that exist before the program is authorized, there are cases (e.g., programs involving public-private partnership or programs involving organizations or work in multiple countries) where the program itself presents unique procurement challenges. A program procurement assessment should be prepared during program definition when procurement presents special challenges or represents a significant level of effort during program delivery.

The output of this activity is the program procurement management assessment, which is an input to the program business case, program charter, and program procurement management planning during program planning.

8.1.1.6 PROGRAM QUALITY ASSESSMENT

An assessment of quality constraints, expectations, risks, and controls should be included as part of program formulation. Organizational or regulatory quality standards may act as important constraints on program delivery, particularly in the case of a compliance program. Expectations about the quality of program outputs may serve as important inputs to determine program costs and required program infrastructure and resources. The ability of program suppliers to comply with quality standards may also be an important consideration for the program procurement and risk assessments. Finally, the need for program quality reviews or audits may be considered important to enable program governance.

The output of this activity is the program quality assessment, which is an input to the program business case, program charter, and program quality management planning during program planning.

8.1.1.7 PROGRAM RESOURCE REQUIREMENTS ESTIMATION

The resources required to plan and deliver a program include people, office space, laboratories, data centers or other facilities, equipment of all types, software, vehicles, and office supplies. An estimate of the required resources—particularly staff and facilities, which may have long lead times or affect ongoing activities—is required to prepare the program business case and should be reflected in the program charter.

The output of this activity is the program resource requirements estimate, which is an input to the program business case, program charter, and program resource management planning during program planning.

8.1.1.8 PROGRAM INITIAL RISK ASSESSMENT

A program risk is an event or series of events or conditions that, if they occur, may affect the success of the program. Positive risks are often referred to as opportunities and negative risks as threats. These risks arise from the program components and their interactions with each other, from technical complexity, schedule or cost constraints, and with the broader environment in which the program is managed.

Two aspects of risk should be assessed during program definition. First, an identification of the key risks that the program may encounter and their relative likelihood and impact should be developed as an input to the program business case and the program charter. Second, an assessment of the organization's willingness to accept and deal with risks—sometimes referred to as its risk appetite—is essential in understanding the level of effort that may be required to monitor and assess risks during program delivery.

The output of this activity is the program initial risk assessment, which is an input to the program business case, the program initial cost estimate, the program charter, the program roadmap, and program risk management planning during program planning.

8.1.1.9 PROGRAM SCHEDULE ASSESSMENT

An assessment of expectations for delivery dates and benefits milestones should be part of the program charter. This initial assessment should also state the level of confidence in the assessment of activity durations and identify where alternative activities could be initiated if activities run into excessive delays.

The output of this activity is the program schedule assessment, which is an input to the program business case, the program charter, the program roadmap, and program schedule management planning during program planning.

8.1.1.10 PROGRAM SCOPE ASSESSMENT

Program scope defines the work required to deliver a benefit (major product, service, or result with specified features and functions) at the program level. Program scope management is the activities that define, develop, monitor, control, and verify program scope. Scope management aligns the program scope with the program's goals and objectives. It includes work decomposition into deliverable component products designed to deliver the associated benefits.

An assessment of program scope, which includes boundaries, links to other programs/projects, and ongoing activities, is required as part of the program charter and to support initial cost, change, resource, risk, and schedule assessments.

This initial program scope assessment develops the program scope statement from the program goals and objectives. This input to the program charter can be obtained from the program sponsor or stakeholders through the portfolio management or stakeholder alignment activities.

The output of this activity is the program scope assessment, which is an input to the program charter.

8.1.2 PROGRAM PLANNING PHASE ACTIVITIES

In program planning, the program organization is defined, and an initial team is deployed to develop the program management plan. The program management plan is developed based on the organization's strategic plan, business case, program charter, and the outputs from the assessments completed during program definition. The plan includes the roadmap of the program components and the management arrangements through which program delivery will be monitored and controlled. The plan should be open for changes, taking into consideration that the success of a program is not measured against its baseline but is measured by how an organization is able to realize benefits from the program outcomes. The program management plan is therefore a reference document and should be seen as a managed baseline.

Figure 8-2 illustrates how program planning activities support development of the program management plan through the core activity of program integration management.

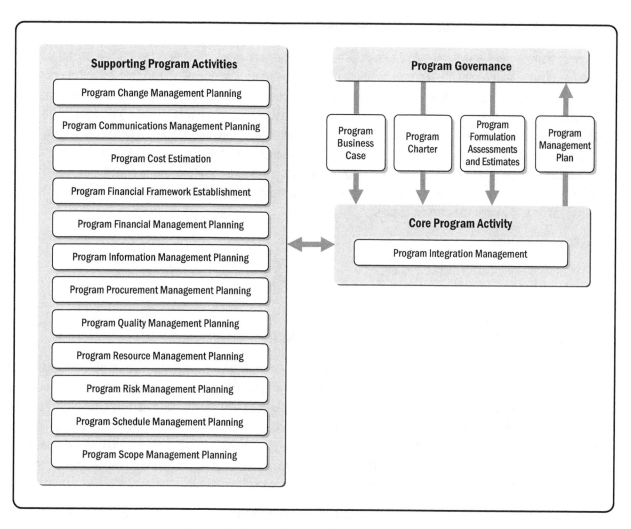

Figure 8-2. Program Planning Phase Activity Interaction

8.1.2.1 PROGRAM CHANGE MANAGEMENT PLANNING

A change management activity should be established to administer changes during the course of the program. The program change management plan is a component of the program management plan that establishes program change management principles and procedures, including the approach for capturing requested changes, evaluating each requested change, determining the disposition of each requested change, communicating a decision to impacted stakeholders, documenting the change request and supporting detail, and authorizing funding and work. It is important to mention that the plan should focus on how to evaluate the impact of a change (e.g., change in a component, change in the roadmap, change in a technology, etc.) to the program outcomes and therefore on the benefits expected by the stakeholders. Based on that assumption, the program steering committee should agree on the level of program change thresholds that should trigger the change process.

The outputs of this activity include:

◆ Program change management plan, and

◆ Program change thresholds.

8.1.2.2 PROGRAM COMMUNICATIONS MANAGEMENT PLANNING

The importance of managing communications internal and external to the program cannot be underestimated or overlooked. Program managers spend a significant amount of time and effort communicating with the program stakeholders, including the program team, component teams, component managers, customers, and program sponsor. Significant problems may occur if sufficient effort is not committed to communications. Program Communications Management includes the activities for the timely and appropriate generation, collection, distribution, storage, retrieval, and ultimate disposition of program information. These activities provide the critical links between people and information that are necessary for successful communications and decision making.

Program communications management planning is the activity of determining the information and communication needs of the program stakeholders based on who needs what information, when they need it, how it will be given to them, and by whom. The program communications management plan is the component of the program management plan that describes how, when, and by whom information will be administered and disseminated. Communication requirements should be clearly defined to facilitate the transfer of information between the program and its components and from the program to the appropriate stakeholders with the appropriate content and delivery methods. Communication requirements specific to particular stakeholders should be included in the stakeholder register.

As the program progresses, other components are added and new stakeholders become known and addressed. This distinction should be considered when planning communications. Cultural and language differences, time zones, and other factors associated with globalization should be considered when developing the program communications management plan. Although complex, program communications management planning is vital to the success of any program.

The outputs of this activity include:

◆ Program communications management plan, and

◆ Communication requirements inputs to the stakeholder register.

8.1.2.3 PROGRAM COST ESTIMATION

Program cost estimating is performed throughout the course of the program. Many organizations use a tiered funding process with a series of go/no-go decisions at each major stage of the program. They agree to an overall financial management plan and commit to a budget only for the next stage at each governance milestone.

A weight or probability may be applied based on the risk and complexity of the work to be performed in order to derive a confidence factor in the estimate. Statistical techniques such as Monte Carlo simulation can also be used. This confidence factor is used to determine the potential range of program costs. When determining program costs, decision makers need to consider not only the development and implementation costs, but also sustainment costs that may occur after the program is completed. Calculating full life cycle costs and including transition and sustainment costs result in total cost of ownership. Total cost of ownership is considered to be relative to the expected benefit of one program against another to derive a funding decision. There are numerous estimating techniques to derive program cost estimates.

Program cost estimates should also identify any critical assumptions upon which the estimates are made, as these assumptions may prove unfounded in the course of program delivery and require reconsideration of the program business case or revision of the program management plan.

Finally, program cost estimation can support or guide cost estimation at the component level. Any prevailing program-level cost estimation guidance intended for use at the component level should be documented and communicated to component managers.

The outputs of this activity include:

◆ Program cost estimates,

◆ Program cost estimation assumptions, and

◆ Component cost estimation guidelines.

8.1.2.4 PROGRAM FINANCIAL FRAMEWORK ESTABLISHMENT

The type of program and the funding structure dictate the financial environment for the duration of the program. Funding models vary, from those that are:

◆ Funded entirely within a single organization,

◆ Managed within a single organization but funded separately,

◆ Funded and managed entirely from outside the parent organization, and

◆ Supported with internal and external sources of funding.

Often the program itself may be funded by one or more sources, and the program components may be funded by altogether different sources. In addition to funding sources, the timing of funding has a direct impact on a program's ability to perform. To a much greater extent than for projects, program costs occur earlier (often years earlier) than their related benefits. The objective of financing in program development is to obtain funds to bridge the gap between paying out monies for development and obtaining the benefits of the programs. Covering this large negative cash balance in the most effective manner is a key challenge in program financing. Due to the large amount of money involved in most programs, the funding organization is rarely a passive partner but instead has significant inputs to program management and to decisions made by the business leads, technical leads, and program manager. Due to this, communications with the program sponsor and other key stakeholders should be proactive and timely.

A program financial framework is a high-level initial plan for coordinating available funding, determining constraints, and determining how funding is allocated. The financial framework defines and describes the program funding flows so that the money is spent as efficiently as possible.

As the program financial framework is developed and analyzed, changes may be identified that impact the original business case justifying the program. Based on these changes, the business case is revised with full involvement of the decision makers (see Section 3.1).

It is important to understand the specific and unique needs of the program sponsor and the funding organizations' representatives with regard to financial arrangements. The program communications management and stakeholder engagement plans may need updates to reflect these needs.

The outputs of this activity include:

- Program financial framework,

- Business case updates, and

- Updates to the program communications management and stakeholder engagement plans.

8.1.2.5 PROGRAM FINANCIAL MANAGEMENT PLANNING

Program financial management comprises the activities related to identifying the program's financial sources and resources, integrating the budgets of the program components, developing the overall budget for the program, and controlling costs during the program. In this context, the program financial management plan is a component of the program management plan that documents all of the program's financial aspects: funding schedules and milestones, initial budget, contract payments and schedules, financial reporting activities and mechanisms, and the financial metrics.

The program financial management plan expands upon the program financial framework and describes the management of items such as risk reserves, potential cash flow problems, international exchange rate fluctuations, future interest rate increases or decreases, inflation, currency devaluation, local laws regarding finances, trends in material costs, and contract incentive and penalty clauses. The plan should include an approval or authorization process to allocate funds for program components. For programs that are funded internally, either through retained earnings, bank loans, or the sale of bonds, the program manager should consider scheduled contract payments, inflation, the aforementioned factors, and other environmental factors. When developing the program financial management plan, the program manager should also include any component payment schedules, operational costs, and infrastructure costs.

Developing the program's initial budget involves compiling all available financial information and listing all income and payment schedules in sufficient detail so that the program's costs can be tracked as part of the program budget. Once baselined, the budget becomes the primary financial target that the program is measured against.

It is important to develop financial metrics by which the program's benefits are measured. This is usually a challenge as cause-effect relationships are often difficult to establish in an endeavor the size and length of a program. One of the tasks of the program team and program steering committee is to establish and validate these financial performance indicators.

As changes to cost, schedule, and scope occur throughout the duration of the program, these metrics are measured against the initial metrics used to approve the program. Decisions to continue, cancel, or modify the program are based, in part, on the results of these financial measures. Program financial risks that are identified as part of the financial management plan should be incorporated into the program risk register.

The outputs of this activity include:

◆ Program financial management plan,

◆ Initial program budget,

◆ Program funding schedules,

◆ Component payment schedules,

◆ Program operational costs,

◆ Inputs to program risk register, and

◆ Program financial metrics.

8.1.2.6 PROGRAM INFORMATION MANAGEMENT PLANNING

The program information management plan is a component of the program management plan that describes how the program's information assets will be prepared, collected, organized, and secured. It is often composed of (but not limited to) information management policies, distribution lists, appropriate tools, templates, and reporting formats. Such information will be gathered and retrieved through a variety of media including manual filing systems, electronic databases, project management software, and systems that allow access to technical documentation such as engineering drawings, design specifications, and test plans. Program information distribution methods are determined once the program's information management system is determined. Information technology allows for rapid dissemination of large amounts of data to a large number of recipients, which requires careful planning and setup of the program's information management system.

The outputs of this activity include:

◆ Program information management plan, and

◆ Program information management tools and templates.

8.1.2.7 PROGRAM PROCUREMENT MANAGEMENT PLANNING

Program procurement management is the application of knowledge, skills, tools, and techniques necessary to acquire products and services to meet the needs of the overall program and the constituent projects/components. Program procurement management planning addresses the activities necessary to acquire products and services and therefore the specific procurement needs that are unique to managing the overall program and the needs of the constituent components. The program procurement management plan is a component of the program management plan that describes how the program will acquire goods and services from outside of the performing organization.

A program manager should understand the resources required for the delivery of benefits expected of the program. Techniques such as make-or-buy decisions and program work-breakdown-structure charts aid in this activity. The program manager needs to be cognizant of the available funding and the needs of all components.

Early and intensive planning is critical for successful program procurement management. Through the planning activity, the program manager looks across all program components and develops a comprehensive plan that optimizes the procurements to meet program objectives and for the delivery of program benefits. To do this, program procurement management addresses commonality and differences for the various procurements across the program scope and determines:

◆ Whether some of the common needs of several individual components could best be met with one overall procurement rather than several separate procurement actions;

◆ The best mix of the types of procurement contracts planned across the program; at the component level, a particular type of contract (e.g., firm-fixed-price) may appear to be the best procurement solution, but a different contract type (e.g., incentive fee) may be optimal for that same procurement when viewed at the program level;

◆ The best program-wide approach to competition (for example, the risks of sole source contracts in one area of the program could be balanced with the different risks associated with full and open competition in other areas of the program);

◆ The best program-wide approach to balancing specific external regulatory mandates; for example, rather than setting aside a certain percentage of each contract in the program to meet a small-business mandate, it may be optimal to award one complete contract to achieve the same mandate.

Often, an analysis of alternatives is performed in the planning stage. This may include requests for information (RFIs), feasibility studies, trade studies, and market analysis to determine the best fit of solutions and services to meet the specific needs of the program.

Due to the inherent need to optimize program procurement management and the requirements to adhere to all legal and financial obligations, it is essential that all personnel responsible for procurement at the component level work closely together, especially during the planning phase.

The outputs of this activity include:

◆ Program procurement standards,

◆ Program procurement management plan, and

◆ Program budget/financial plan updates.

8.1.2.8 PROGRAM QUALITY MANAGEMENT PLANNING

Program quality management planning identifies the organizational or regulatory quality standards that are relevant to the program as a whole and specifies how to satisfy them across the program. The program quality management plan is a component of the program management plan that describes how an organization's quality policies will be implemented. Often within a program, there are many differing quality assurance requirements as well as differing test and quality control methods and activities. Program quality management is the activities of the performing organization that determine program quality policies, objectives, and responsibilities so that the program will be successful. Program quality management aims to align these varying requirements and control methods, and may add additional ones to ensure overall program quality. It is good practice for the program manager to document the overall program's quality objectives and principles in a quality policy that is shared with all program components.

Program management is responsible for the planning of the proper quality assurance criteria throughout the life cycle of the program, which may in fact exceed the timeline of the individual components. New quality control tools, activities, and techniques may be introduced into the program and employed when appropriate; for example, when new laws are enacted or new components are introduced during the program's life cycle.

When initiating the program, the cost of the level of quality requirements should be evaluated and incorporated into the business plan. Quality is a variable cost in all components and should be considered as such in the program quality management plan. It is beneficial to analyze program quality in order to evaluate it across the program with the goal of combining quality tests and inspections in order to reduce costs, where feasible. If the tests are not coordinated, products and deliverables could be tested several times throughout a program and a cost incurred for no valid reason. It should be noted that the output of this activity is a quality management plan that provides the quality assurance measures and quality controls that are incorporated in the program and the methods of inspection based on the program scope.

Quality management should be considered when defining all program management activity as well as for every deliverable and service. For example, when developing a program resource management plan, it is recommended that a program quality manager participate in the planning activity to verify that quality activities and controls are applied and flow down to all the components, including those performed by subcontractors.

The output of this activity is a program quality management plan that may contain:

◆ Program quality policy;

◆ Program quality standards;

◆ Program quality estimates of costs;

◆ Quality metrics, service level agreements, or memorandums of understanding;

◆ Quality checklists; and

◆ Quality assurance and control specifications.

8.1.2.9 PROGRAM RESOURCE MANAGEMENT PLANNING

Resource management at the program level is different from resource management at the component level; a program manager needs to work within the bounds of uncertainty and balance the needs of the components for which he or she is responsible. Program resource management ensures all required resources (people, equipment, material, etc.) are made available to the component managers to enable the delivery of benefits for the program.

Resource management planning involves identifying existing resources and the need for additional resources. In the case of human resources, the sum of resources needed to successfully complete each component can be less than the total quantity of resources needed to complete the program because the resources can be reallocated between components as the components are completed. The program manager analyzes the availability of each resource, in terms of both capacity and capability, and determines how these resources will be allocated across components to avoid overcommitment or inadequate support. Historical information may be used to determine the types of resources that were required for similar projects and programs.

The resource management plan is a component of the program management plan that forecasts the expected level of resource use across the program components and relative to the program master schedule to allow the program manager to identify potential resource shortfalls or conflicts over the use of scarce or constrained resources. The plan also describes the guidelines for making program resource prioritization decisions and resolving resource conflicts.

When resources are unavailable within the program, the program manager calls upon the larger organization for assistance. When necessary, the program manager should work with the organization to develop a statement of work (SOW) to contract the necessary resources.

The outputs of this activity include:

◆ Program resource requirements, and

◆ Program resource management plan.

8.1.2.10 PROGRAM RISK MANAGEMENT PLANNING

Program risk management planning identifies how to approach and conduct risk management activities for a program by considering its components. The principles for risk management should be applied as outlined in the *Practice Standard for Project Risk Management* [8]. The risk management plan is a component of the program management plan that describes how risk management activities will be structured and performed.

Planning risk management activities ensures that the level, type, and visibility of risk management are appropriate, based on the risks and importance of the program to the organization. It identifies the resources and time required for risk management activities. In addition, it establishes an agreed-upon basis for evaluating risks.

The program risk management planning activity should be conducted early in the program definition phase. It is crucial for the successful performance of other activities described in this section. It may also need to be repeated whenever major changes occur in the program. A key output of this activity is the program risk register, which is the document in which risks are recorded together with the results of risk analysis and risk response planning. The program risk register is a living document that is updated as program risks and risk responses change during program delivery.

It is essential to define risk profiles of organizations to construct the most suitable approach to managing program risks, adjusting risk sensitivity, and monitoring risk criticality. Risk targets and risk thresholds influence the program management plan. Risk profiles may be expressed in policy statements or revealed in actions. These actions may highlight organizational willingness to embrace high-threat situations or a reluctance to forgo high-opportunity choices. Market factors that apply to the program and to its components should be included as an environmental factor. Culture of the organization and stakeholders also plays a role in shaping the approach to risk management.

Organizations may have predefined approaches to risk management such as risk categories, common definition of concepts and terms, risk statement formats, standard templates, roles and responsibilities, and authority levels for decision making. Lessons learned from executing similar programs in the past are also critical assets to be reviewed as a component of establishing an effective risk management plan.

The outputs from this activity include:

◆ Program risk management plan, and

◆ Program risk register.

8.1.2.11 PROGRAM SCHEDULE MANAGEMENT PLANNING

The program schedule management activity determines the order and timing of the components needed to produce the program benefits, estimates the amount of time required to accomplish each one, identifies significant milestones during the performance of the program, and documents the outcomes of each milestone. Typically, a program schedule is developed collaboratively with components as component schedules are elaborated. Program components include projects, subsidiary programs, and other work undertaken to deliver the program's scope.

Program schedule management planning begins with the program scope management plan and the program work breakdown structure (WBS), which defines how the program components are expected to deliver the program's outputs and benefits. The initial program master schedule is often created before the detailed schedules of the individual components are available. The program's delivery date and major milestones are developed using the program roadmap and the program charter.

The program master schedule is the top-level program planning document that defines the individual component schedules and dependencies among program components (individual components and program-level activities) required to achieve the program goals. It should include those component milestones that represent an output to the program or share interdependency with other components.

The program master schedule should also include activities that are unique to the program including, but not limited to, activities related to stakeholder engagement, program-level risk mitigation, and program-level reviews. The program master schedule determines the timing of individual components, enables the program manager to determine when benefits will be delivered by the program, and identifies external dependencies of the program. The first draft of a program master schedule often only identifies the order and start/end dates of components and their key interdependencies with other components. Later, it may be enriched with more intermediate component results as the component schedules are developed.

Once the high-level program master schedule is determined, the dates for each individual component are identified and used to develop the component's schedule. These dates often act as a constraint at the component level. When a component has multiple deliverables upon which other components rely, those deliverables and interdependencies should be reflected in the overall program master schedule. When a program is established over a set of existing components, the program master schedule needs to incorporate the milestones and deliverables from the individual component schedules.

The schedule model principles outlined in the *Practice Standard for Scheduling* – Second Edition [9] should also be applied to the program master schedule. Maintaining a logic-based program network diagram and monitoring the critical path for component outputs with interdependencies is essential to effective management of the program master schedule, while focusing on benefits realization based on deliverables along the critical path.

The program schedule management plan is a component of the program management plan that establishes the criteria and the activities for developing, monitoring, and controlling the schedule. The program schedule management plan should include guidance on how changes to schedule baselines are to be coordinated and controlled across program components. The program master schedule identifies the agreed-upon sequence of component deliverables to facilitate effective planning of the individual component deliveries and of expected benefits. It provides the program team/stakeholders with a visual representation of how the program is going to be delivered through its life cycle. The program master schedule is a living document and provides the program manager with a mechanism to identify risks and escalate component issues that may affect the program goals.

Program schedule risk inputs that are identified as part of the program master schedule development should be incorporated into the program risk register. These risks may be a result of component dependencies within the schedule or on external factors identified as a result of the agreed-upon program schedule management plan. The program schedule management plan may establish scheduling standards that apply to all program components.

The program roadmap should periodically be assessed and updated to ensure alignment between the program roadmap and the program master schedule. Changes in the program master schedule may require changes in the program roadmap, and changes in the program roadmap should be reflected in the program master schedule.

The outputs of this activity include:

◆ Program schedule management plan,

◆ Program master schedule,

◆ Inputs to the program risk register, and

◆ Updates to the program roadmap.

8.1.2.12 PROGRAM SCOPE MANAGEMENT PLANNING

Program scope management planning includes all of the activities involved in planning and aligning the program scope with the program's goals and objectives. It includes work decomposition into deliverable component products designed to deliver the associated benefits. The objective is to develop a detailed program scope statement, break down the program work into deliverable components, and develop a plan for managing the scope throughout the program.

Program scope is typically described in the form of expected benefits but may also be described as user stories or scenarios depending on the type of program. Program scope encompasses all benefits to be delivered by the program, which are reflected in the form of a program WBS.

A program WBS is a deliverable-oriented hierarchical decomposition encompassing the total scope of the program, and it includes the deliverables to be produced by the constituent components. Elements not in the program WBS are outside the scope of the program. The program WBS includes, but is not limited to, program management artifacts such as plans, procedures, standards, processes, program management deliverables, and program management office (PMO) support deliverables. The program WBS provides an overview of the program and shows how each component contributes to the objectives of the program. Decomposition stops at the level of control required by the program manager (typically to the first one or two levels of a component). The program WBS serves as the framework for developing the program master schedule and defines the program manager's management control points. It is an essential tool for building realistic schedules, developing cost estimates, and organizing work. It also provides the framework for reporting, tracking, and controlling.

Program-level deliverables should be clearly linked to benefits and focus on those activities associated with stakeholder engagement, program-level management (as opposed to management within its components), and component oversight and integration. Program scope includes scope that is decomposed and allocated into components. Care should be taken to avoid decomposing component-level scope into details that overlap the component managers' responsibilities.

Once the scope is developed, a plan for managing, documenting, and communicating scope changes should be developed during the program definition phase. The program scope management plan is a component of the program management plan that describes how the scope will be defined, developed, monitored, controlled, and verified.

The outputs of this activity include:

◆ Program scope statement,

◆ Program scope management plan, and

◆ Program work breakdown structure (WBS).

8.2 PROGRAM DELIVERY PHASE ACTIVITIES

Program delivery phase activities include program activities required for coordinating and managing the actual delivery of programs. These include activities around change control, reporting, and information distribution as well as activities around cost, procurement, quality, and risk.

These provide supporting activities and processes that run throughout the program life cycle and are aimed to provide the program monitoring and controlling functions. Figure 8-3 illustrates how program delivery activities support program and component management.

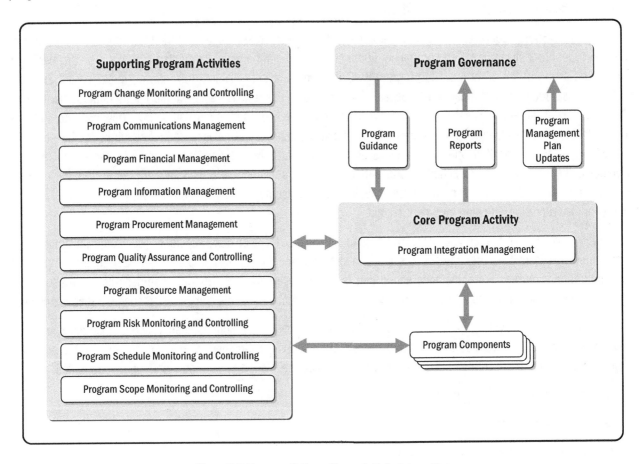

Figure 8-3. Program Delivery Phase Activity Interaction

8.2.1 PROGRAM CHANGE MONITORING AND CONTROLLING

Program change monitoring and controlling are the activities whereby modifications to documents, deliverables, or baselines associated with the program are identified, documented, approved, or rejected. Program change monitoring and controlling is a critical aspect of overall program delivery monitoring and controlling and should include monitoring factors internal and external to the program that might create the need for changes to the program.

A program change request is a formal proposal to modify any program document, deliverable, or baseline. Program change requests should be recorded in the program change log. The program change requests should be analyzed to determine their urgency and impact on program baseline elements and other program components. When there are multiple ways to implement the change, the costs, risks, and other aspects of each option should be assessed to enable selection of the approach most likely to deliver the program's intended benefits.

Once a decision on the program change request has been made by the program manager or program steering committee, program change control should ensure that the request is:

◆ Recorded in the program change log;

◆ Communicated to appropriate stakeholders, according to the program communications management plan; and

◆ Reflected in updates to component plans, as warranted.

The outputs of this activity include:

◆ Approved change requests, and

◆ Updates to the program change log.

8.2.2 PROGRAM COMMUNICATIONS MANAGEMENT

Program communications management comprises the activities necessary for the timely and appropriate generation, collection, distribution, storage, retrieval, and ultimate disposition of program information. Program communications management includes coordination, direction, and support of component communications to ensure alignment with the program's overall communications objectives. Program information is distributed to the receiving parties including the clients, program sponsor, program steering committee, component managers, and, in some cases, the public and press.

The outputs of this activity include program communications regarding:

◆ Status information on the program, projects, subsidiary programs, or other work, including progress, cost information, risk analysis, and other information relevant to internal or external audiences;

◆ Notification of program change requests to the program and component teams, and the corresponding response to the change requests;

◆ Program financial reports for internal or external stakeholders or for the purpose of public disclosure;

◆ External filings with government and regulatory bodies as prescribed by laws and regulations;

◆ Presentations before legislative bodies with the required prebriefs;

◆ Public announcements communicating public outreach information;

◆ Press releases; and

◆ Media interviews and benefits updates.

8.2.2.1 PROGRAM INFORMATION DISTRIBUTION METHODS

Program information is distributed using a variety of methods, including:

◆ Face-to-face meetings and presentations to groups of stakeholders or program team members;

◆ Electronic communications and conferencing tools, such as email, fax, voicemail, telephone, video and web conferencing, and web publishing;

◆ Electronic tools for program management, such as web interfaces to scheduling and project management software, meeting and virtual office support software, portals, and collaborative work management tools;

◆ Social media (internet-based group communication tools), interviews, conference presentations, marketing, publication articles; and

◆ Informal communications such as emails, small group conversations, and staff meetings. These are the primary methods for communicating day-to-day activities but are not used to formally communicate the program's status.

Regardless of the distribution method, the information should remain in the program's control. An incorrect message to an audience may cause problems for the program and in some cases lead to the stoppage of a program. Program Communications Management can be challenging and time-consuming and may require a full-time manager assigned to the task.

8.2.2.2 PROGRAM REPORTING

Program reporting is a critical element of program communications, as it supports both program governance and stakeholder engagement. Program reporting is the activity of consolidating performance and reporting related data to provide stakeholders with information about how resources are being used to deliver program benefits. Program reporting aggregates all information across projects, subsidiary programs, and program activities to provide a clear picture of the program as a whole.

This information is conveyed to the stakeholders by means of the information distribution activity to provide them with needed status and deliverable information. Additionally, this information is communicated to program team members and its constituent components to provide them with general and background information about the program. Communication should be a two-way information flow. Any communications from customers or stakeholders regarding the program should be gathered by program management, analyzed, and distributed back within the program as required.

The outputs of this activity include:

◆ Reports required by program sponsors or program agreements, including formats and reporting frequency,

◆ Customer feedback requests, and

◆ Periodic reports and presentations.

8.2.3 PROGRAM FINANCIAL MANAGEMENT

Once the program receives initial funding and begins paying expenses, the financial effort moves into tracking, monitoring, and controlling the program's funds and expenditures.

Monitoring the program's finances and controlling expenditures within budget are critical aspects of ensuring the program meets the goals of the funding agency or of the higher organization. A program whose costs exceed the planned budget may no longer satisfy the business case used to justify it and may be subject to cancellation. Even minor overruns are subject to audit and management oversight and should be justified. Typical financial management activities include:

◆ Identifying factors that create changes to the budget baseline,

◆ Monitoring the environmental factors for potential impacts,

◆ Managing changes when they occur,

◆ Monitoring costs reallocation impact and results among components,

◆ Monitoring contract expenditures to ensure funds are disbursed in accordance with the contracts,

◆ Implementing earned value management (schedule performance index, cost performance index),

◆ Identifying impacts to the program components from overruns or underruns,

◆ Communicating changes to the budget baseline to the governance groups and to the auditors (at both the program and component levels), and

◆ Managing the expenditure on the program infrastructure to ensure costs are within expected parameters.

As part of this activity, payments are made in accordance with the contracts, with the financial infrastructure of the program, and with the status of the contract deliverables. Individual component budgets are closed when work is completed on each component. Throughout the program, as changes are approved that have significant cost impacts, the program's budget baseline is updated accordingly and the budget is rebaselined. New financial forecasts for the program are prepared on a regular basis and communicated in accordance with the program communications management plan. Similarly, approved changes either to the program or to an individual component are incorporated into the appropriate budget. All of these activities may result in updates to the program management plan.

The outputs of this activity include:

◆ Contract payments,

◆ Closed component budgets,

◆ Program budget baseline updates,

◆ Approved change requests,

◆ Revised estimate at completion,

◆ Program management plan updates, and

◆ Corrective actions.

8.2.3.1 PROGRAM COST BUDGETING

Since programs are, by definition, composed of multiple components, program budgets should include the costs for each individual component as well as costs for the resources to manage the program itself. The baselined program budget is the primary financial target that the program is measured against. The majority of the program's cost is attributable to the individual components within the program and not to managing the program itself. When contractors are involved, the details of the budget come from the contracts. The cost of program management and supporting program activities is added to the initial budget figure before a baseline budget can be prepared.

Two important parts of the budget are program payment schedules and component payment schedules. The program payment schedules identify the schedules and milestones where funding is received from the funding organization. The component payment schedules indicate how and when contractors are paid in accordance with the contract provisions. Once the baseline is determined, the program management plan is updated.

The outputs of this activity include:

◆ Updates to the program budget baseline,

◆ Program payment schedules, and

◆ Component payment schedules.

8.2.3.2 COMPONENT COST ESTIMATION

Because programs have a significant element of uncertainty, not all program components may be known when the initial order-of-magnitude estimates are calculated during the program definition phase. In addition, given the typically long duration of a program, the initial estimates may need to be updated to reflect the current environment and cost considerations. It is a generally accepted good practice to calculate an estimate as close to the beginning of a work effort as possible. This way, if the cost of the output is lower than originally planned, the program manager may present an opportunity to the program sponsor for additional products that would be acquired later in the program. Conversely, if the cost is significantly higher, a change request may be generated. In the approval activity, the benefit of additional products can be weighed against the new cost to determine the proper action.

Cost estimates for the individual components within the program are developed. The component costs are baselined and become the budget for that particular component. When a contractor is performing this component, this cost is written into the contract.

The outputs of this activity include component cost estimates.

8.2.4 PROGRAM INFORMATION MANAGEMENT

Effective program management involves the extensive exchange of information among program management, component management, portfolio management, program stakeholders, and program governance functions of an organization. Managing this information and making it available to support program communications, program management, or archiving is a significant and continuous task, especially in organizations pursuing numerous programs or programs that are complicated or complex.

Using the information management tools and processes established in the program information management plan, this activity collects, receives, organizes, and stores the documents and other information products created by program activities, program governance, and program components. Attention should be paid to the accuracy and timeliness of the information to avoid errors and incorrect decisions. The program information repository can be an invaluable aid to other program activities, particularly when there is a need to refer to past decisions or prepare analyses based on trends reflected in historical program information.

The outputs of this activity include:

◆ Updates to the program information repository, and

◆ Inputs to information distribution and program reporting.

8.2.4.1 LESSONS LEARNED DATABASE

Lessons learned are a compilation of knowledge gained. This knowledge may be acquired from executing similar and relevant programs in the past, or it may reside in public domain databases. Lessons learned are critical assets to be reviewed when updating the program stakeholder register, program risk register, and program communications management plan or when considering major changes to the program management plan, including the introduction of new program components. The lessons learned database is updated when necessary, including at the completion of components and at the end of the program.

The outputs of this activity include:

◆ Lessons learned reports,

◆ Inputs to program stakeholder register and risk register updates,

◆ Inputs to program communications management plan updates, and

◆ Inputs to program management plan changes.

8.2.5 PROGRAM PROCUREMENT MANAGEMENT

Program managers utilize multiple tools and techniques to conduct program procurements, but the key objective of conducting program-level procurement is to set standards for the components. These standards may come in the form of qualified seller lists, pre-negotiated contracts, blanket purchase agreements, and formalized proposal evaluation criteria.

One common structure used by the program manager is to direct all procurements to be centralized and conducted by a program-level team rather than assigning that responsibility to individual components.

The outputs of this activity include:

◆ Request for quote (RFQ),

◆ Request for proposal (RFP),

◆ Invitation for bid (IFB),

◆ Proposal evaluation criteria,

◆ Agreements administration plan, and

◆ Signed agreements.

8.2.5.1 PROGRAM CONTRACT ADMINISTRATION

Once the program standards are in place and the agreements are signed, administration and closeout of many contracts are transitioned to the components. The details of contract deliverables, requirements, deadlines, cost, and quality are handled at the component level. The individual managers at the component level report procurement results and closeouts to the program manager. Where contracts are administered at the program level, however, component managers coordinate or report deliverable acceptance, contract changes, and other contract issues with the program staff.

The program manager maintains visibility in the procurements to ensure the program budget is being expended properly to obtain program benefits.

The outputs of this activity include:

◆ Performance/earned value reports,

◆ Ongoing progress reports, and

◆ Vendor/contract performance reports.

8.2.6 PROGRAM QUALITY ASSURANCE AND CONTROL

Program quality assurance and control involves the activities related to the periodic evaluation of overall program quality to provide confidence that the program will comply with relevant quality policies and standards. Once the initial quality assurance specifications are decided upon in the program planning subphase, quality should be continuously monitored and analyzed. Programs often conduct quality assurance audits to ensure proper updates are performed. New government laws and regulations may create new quality standards. The program management team is responsible for implementing all required quality changes. The lengthy duration of programs often requires quality assurance updates throughout the program's duration. Program quality assurance focuses on cross-program, intercomponent quality relationships and how one component's quality specification impacts another component's quality, when they are interdependent. Program quality assurance also includes the analysis of the quality control results of the program components to ensure overall program quality is delivered.

The outputs from this activity may include:

◆ Quality assurance audit findings, and

◆ Quality assurance change requests.

8.2.6.1 PROGRAM QUALITY CONTROL

Program quality control involves the monitoring of specific components or program deliverables and results to determine if they meet the quality requirements and lead to benefits realization. The quality control activity ensures that quality plans are implemented at project and subsidiary program levels, using quality reviews usually performed with constituent component reviews. Quality control is performed throughout the duration of the program. Program results include product and service deliverables, management results and cost schedule, and performance, as well as benefits realized by the end user. End-user satisfaction is a powerful metric that should be obtained to gauge the program quality. The fitness for use of the benefits, product, or service delivered by the program is best evaluated by those who receive it. To that end, programs often use customer satisfaction surveys as a quality control measurement.

Outputs from this activity may include:

◆ Quality change requests,

◆ Quality control completed checklists and inspection reports, and

◆ Quality test reports or measurement results.

8.2.7 PROGRAM RESOURCE MANAGEMENT

Throughout program delivery, the program manager will need to monitor, control, and adapt program resources to ensure benefits delivery. Resource prioritization allows the program manager to prioritize the use of resources that are not available in abundance and to optimize their use across all components within the program. This often involves human resource planning to identify, document, and assign program roles and responsibilities to individuals or groups.

During program delivery, the need for staff, facilities, equipment, and other resources change. These fluctuations are similar to the economics of supply and demand. The program manager manages resources at the program level and works with the component managers who manage resources at the component level to balance the needs of the program with the availability of resources.

Resource prioritization decisions should be based on the guidelines in the program resource management plan. As decisions to change existing program components or to initiate new ones may have impacts on program resources, the program resource management plan may need to be adapted as a result.

The outputs of this activity include:

◆ Program resource prioritization decisions, and

◆ Updates to the program resource management plan.

8.2.7.1 RESOURCE INTERDEPENDENCY MANAGEMENT

Resources are often shared among different components within a program, and the program manager should work to ensure that the interdependencies do not cause delay in benefits delivery. This is achieved by carefully controlling the schedule for scarce resources. The program manager ensures resources are released for other programs when they are no longer necessary for the current program.

The program manager may work with the component managers to ensure the program resource management plan accounts for changes in use of interdependent or scarce program resources.

The output of this activity includes updates to the program resource management plan.

8.2.8 PROGRAM RISK MONITORING AND CONTROLLING

Throughout program delivery, program risk management will monitor and control program risks through:

◆ Program risk identification,

◆ Program risk analysis, and

◆ Program risk response management.

Risk monitoring is also conducted to determine whether:

◆ Program assumptions are still valid;

◆ Assessed risk has changed from its prior state, with analysis of trends;

◆ Proper risk management policies and procedures are being followed; and

◆ Cost or schedule contingency reserves are modified in line with the risks of the program.

Effective program risk monitoring and controlling also requires coordination with component risk management functions.

8.2.8.1 PROGRAM RISK IDENTIFICATION

The program risk identification activity determines which risks could affect the program, documents their characteristics, and prepares for their successful management. Participants in risk identification activities may include the program manager, program sponsor, program team members, risk management team, subject matter experts from outside the program team, customers, end users, component managers, managers of other program components, stakeholders, risk management experts, and external reviewers, as required.

Risk identification is an iterative activity. As the program progresses, new risks may evolve or become known. The frequency of iteration and involvement of participants may vary, but the format of the risk statements should be consistent. This allows for the comparison of risk events in the program. The identification activity should provide sufficient information to allow the risk to be analyzed and prioritized.

The output of this activity may include updates to the program risk register.

8.2.8.2 PROGRAM RISK ANALYSIS

Risk analysis at the program level should integrate relevant program component risks. Managing the interdependencies among the component risks and the program provides significant benefits to the program and its components.

Qualitative and quantitative risk analysis techniques are both useful to support program management decisions. This step in the risk management activity produces the best information supporting the contingency reserve and management reserve that should be set aside to deal with risks that actually occur. The assessments should include costs, schedules, and performance outcomes for the components as well as their interdependencies.

The impact of the negative risks (threats) and positive risks (opportunities) on the delivery of benefits to the organization or external stakeholders should be considered at the program level. One essential difference between programs and components is the time scale; component-level risks should be dealt with within a relatively short time frame (i.e., at the end of a phase or a component), while program risks may be applicable at a point in the potentially distant future.

The outputs of this activity may include:

◆ Proposed risk responses,

◆ Updates to the program risk register, and

◆ Periodic risk reports showing threat and opportunity trends.

8.2.8.3 PROGRAM RISK RESPONSE MANAGEMENT

To respond to risks, the program manager identifies and directs actions to mitigate the negative consequences or to enable realization of potential benefits. The program manager may hold contingency reserves at the program level to support risk responses. The program contingency reserve is not a substitute for the component contingency reserve, which is held at the component level.

Based on the program manager's direction, components of the program risk register may be updated, including:

◆ Specific actions to implement the chosen response strategy;

◆ Budget and schedule activities required to implement the chosen responses;

◆ Contingency plans and trigger conditions that call for their execution;

◆ Fallback plans for use as a response to a risk that has occurred and the primary response proves to be inadequate;

◆ Residual risks that are expected to remain after planned responses have been taken, as well as those that have been deliberately accepted; and

◆ Secondary risks that arise as a direct outcome of implementing the risk response.

The outputs of this activity may include:

◆ Direction to implement risk responses,

◆ Program risk register updates,

◆ Contingency reserve and management reserve, and

◆ Change requests.

8.2.9 PROGRAM SCHEDULE MONITORING AND CONTROLLING

Program schedule monitoring and controlling is the activity of ensuring the program produces the required capabilities and benefits on time. This activity includes tracking and monitoring the start and finish of all high-level component and program activities and milestones against the program master schedule planned timelines. Updating the program master schedule and directing changes to individual component schedules is required to maintain an accurate and up-to-date program master schedule.

Program schedule monitoring and controlling works closely with other program activities to identify variances to the schedules and directs corrective action when necessary and as described in Section 7.2.2.2. Successful program management is dependent on the alignment of program scope with cost and schedule, which are dependent on each other. Schedule control involves identifying not only slippages but also opportunities to accelerate program or component schedules and should be used for proper risk management. Program schedule risks should be tracked as part of the risk management activity.

The program master schedule should also be reviewed to assess the impact of component-level changes on other components and on the program itself. There may be a need to accelerate or decelerate components within the schedule to achieve program goals. Identification of both slippages and early deliveries are necessary as part of the overall program management function. Identification of early deliveries may provide opportunities for program acceleration. Approval of deviations to component schedules may be necessary to realize program benefits as a result of component performance deviations. Due to the complexity and potential long duration of programs, the program master schedule may need to be updated to include new components or remove components as a result of approved change requests to meet evolving program goals. The program roadmap should be assessed for potential revision when there is significant change in the program master schedule.

The program schedule monitoring and controlling activity include updates to the program master schedule, updates to the program roadmap, and identification of schedule risks as outputs to the activity.

The outputs of this activity may include:

◆ Updates to the program master schedule,

◆ Updates to the program risk register, and

◆ Updates to the program roadmap.

8.2.10 PROGRAM SCOPE MONITORING AND CONTROLLING

It is important for the program manager to monitor and control scope as the program develops in order to ensure successful completion. Scope changes that have significant impact on a component or the program may originate from stakeholders, components within the program, previously unidentified requirements issues, or external sources.

Program scope monitoring and controlling should be exercised in line with the program change management and program scope management plans. This activity should capture requested scope changes, evaluate each requested change, determine the disposition of each requested change, communicate the decision to affected stakeholders, and record the change request and supporting detail. Major change requests, when approved, may require updates to the program management plan and program scope statement.

The program manager is responsible for determining which components of the program are affected when a program scope change is requested and should update the program work breakdown structure accordingly. In very large programs, the number of components affected may be substantial and difficult to assess. Program managers should restrict their activities to managing scope only to the allocated level for components and should avoid controlling component scope that has been further decomposed by the project manager or by subsidiary program managers.

The outputs of this activity may include:

◆ Updated program scope statement,

◆ Dispositions of requests with documentation of the rationale for the decision,

◆ Updates to the program management plan, and

◆ Updates to the program work breakdown structure.

8.3 PROGRAM CLOSURE PHASE ACTIVITIES

The program closure phase activities begin when the program components have delivered all their outputs and the program has begun to deliver its intended benefits. In some cases, program governance may decide to bring a program to an early close before all components have been completed. In either case, the goal of the program activities during this phase is to release the program resources and support the transition of any remaining program outputs and assets, including its documents and databases, to ongoing organizational activities.

Figure 8-4 illustrates how program closure activities support program closure and transition to sustaining organizational operations.

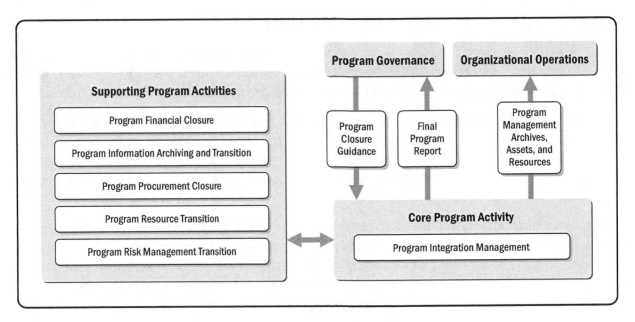

Figure 8-4. Program Closure Phase Activity Interaction

8.3.1 PROGRAM FINANCIAL CLOSURE

To enable program closeout, estimates may be required to determine the costs of sustaining benefits created by the program. While many of these costs are captured in operations, maintenance, or other activities initiated in the program delivery phase as components are delivered, there may be residual activities required to oversee the ongoing benefits. This stewardship may be structured as an individual project or as a resulting program, or may be incorporated as new work under a separate portfolio or program or in new or existing operations. As the program nears completion, the program budget is closed and the final financial reports are communicated in accordance with the program communications management plan. Any unspent monies are returned to the funding organization.

Program financial transition is complete once sustainment budgets are developed, benefits are delivered, and sustainment has commenced.

The outputs of this activity may include:

◆ Input to the program final report,

◆ Updates to the program financial management plan,

◆ Inputs into the knowledge repository,

◆ Documentation of new tools and techniques used in the course of the program into the knowledge management system,

◆ Financial closing statements, and

◆ Closed program budget.

8.3.2 PROGRAM INFORMATION ARCHIVING AND TRANSITION

For legal reasons or to support ensuing operations or other programs, there may be a need to collect program records and organize them for archiving or for use by other elements of the organization. The scope of this activity may include collection and archiving of records and documentation from components as well.

Proper information management during program closure also includes the transfer of program knowledge to support the ongoing sustainment of program benefits by providing the new supporting organization with documentation, training, or materials. The program manager may assess the program's performance, collect observations from program team members, and provide a final lessons learned report that incorporates the individual findings from continuous lessons learned captured throughout the program/component activities. This report can inform the governance and management of other programs in the organization and to help them avoid pitfalls encountered during program delivery.

The outputs of this activity include:

◆ Inputs to organizational archives, and

◆ Lessons learned report to organizational governance bodies.

8.3.3 PROGRAM PROCUREMENT CLOSURE

Program procurement closure activities are those that formally close out each agreement of the program after ensuring that all deliverables have been satisfactorily completed, that all payments have been made, and that there are no outstanding contractual issues. In the case of a program that is closed early, program procurement closure manages the termination of active contracts to avoid unnecessary costs.

The outputs of this activity include:

◆ Contract closeout reports,

◆ Updates to lessons learned, and

◆ Closed contracts.

8.3.4 PROGRAM RESOURCE TRANSITION

It is important to ensure that program resources are appropriately released as the program is being closed. This may involve the reallocation or reassignment of team members and funding to other initiatives or programs. Reassignment of resources at the component level could include transitioning resources to another component already in execution or another program within the organization that requires a similar skill set. Refer to the *PMBOK® Guide* for more information regarding resource disposition for component projects.

Efficient and appropriate release of program resources is an essential activity of program closure. At the program level, program governance releases resources as a part of activities leading to program closure approval.

The outputs of this activity include resources released to other organizational elements.

8.3.5 PROGRAM RISK MANAGEMENT TRANSITION

Although the program is closed, there may be remaining risks that could undermine the realization of benefits by the organization. Program risk management activities should transfer these risks, along with any supporting analysis and response information, to the appropriate organizational risk register. This may be managed by a different organizational group than the one intended to realize the benefits, such as an organizational PMO.

The outputs of this activity include inputs to other organizational risk registers.

REFERENCES

[1]   Project Management Institute. 2017. *A Guide to the Project Management Body of Knowledge (PMBOK® Guide) –* Sixth Edition. Newtown Square, PA: Author.

[2]   Project Management Institute. 2013. *The Standard for Portfolio Management –* Third Edition. Newtown Square, PA: Author.

[3]   Project Management Institute. 2014. *Implementing Organizational Project Management: A Practice Guide –* Third Edition. Newtown Square, PA: Author.

[4]   Project Management Institute. 2015. *PMI Lexicon of Project Management Terms* (Version 3.1). Available from www.pmi.org/lexiconterms.

[5]   Project Management Institute. 2006. *Code of Ethics and Professional Conduct.* Available from www.pmi.org/codeofethicsPDF.

[6]   Project Management Institute. 2013. *Managing Change in Organizations: A Practice Guide.* Newtown Square, PA: Author.

[7]   Project Management Institute. 2016. *Governance of Portfolios, Programs, and Projects: A Practice Guide.* Newtown Square, PA: Author.

[8]   Project Management Institute. 2009. *Practice Standard for Project Risk Management.* Newtown Square, PA: Author.

[9]   Project Management Institute. 2011. *Practice Standard for Scheduling –* Second Edition. Newtown Square, PA: Author.

APPENDIX X1
FOURTH EDITION CHANGES

X1.1 ABOUT THIS APPENDIX

To fully understand the changes that have been made to the structure and content of *The Standard for Program Management* – Fourth Edition, it is important for the reader to be aware of the update committee's objectives as well as the evolution of the standard.

Through the process of updating the Third edition of the standard, it became clear that the growing importance of program management as an organizational competency was generating an increasing demand for clearer lines of distinction between *The Standard for Program Management* and PMI's other core standards, including *A Guide to the Project Management Body of Knowledge (PMBOK® Guide)*, and *The Standard for Portfolio Management*. It was also at this time that the document shifted from a process-based standard to a principle-based standard. The Fourth edition team continued down a similar path, and focused primarily on fine tuning the principles and concepts that make up the standard, as well as ensuring consistency with other foundational standards and applicable practice standards and practice guides.

X1.2 OBJECTIVES

Specifically, the update committee's objectives included:

◆ Maintain the standard as a principle-based document that describes the fundamentals that shape program management and what constitutes good practice on most programs most of the time.

◆ Update the content to reflect current program management accepted practices.

◆ Ensure that the updates interlink and harmonize with other PMI standards as appropriate.

X1.3 APPROACH

To prepare the current update, the project committee developed an approach to the revision that incorporated a number of important strategies and principles, including format and layout (Section X1.3.1) and program management content (Section X1.3.2).

X1.3.1 FORMAT AND LAYOUT

When first encountering *The Standard for Program Management* – Fourth Edition, readers will immediately notice fundamental modifications that have been made to the format and layout of the standard. There are a number of important factors that were considered during the design of the framework for the Fourth Edition that will be beneficial as background information for readers familiar with earlier editions, and will help explain the transition from the format of the Third Edition to the current. To explain the current framework, a brief summary of the evolution of the standard from the first edition to the present is provided:

- ◆ **First Edition.** When it was published, the First edition of *The Standard for Program Management* presented three key themes that captured the prevailing understanding of program management work. These themes included Stakeholder Management, Program Governance, and Benefits Management. Accompanying the themes was the definition of the program management life cycle. This life cycle was integrated into the initial chapters of the standard and further elaborated on in the later chapters. This framework presents a decidedly "domain-oriented" approach to the standard; to the definition of program management work; and to the role of the program manager.

- ◆ **Second Edition.** The Second edition of *The Standard for Program Management* retained some discussion of the three program management themes described in the First edition. Many of the updates, however, focused on expanding the presence of the program management life cycle. This approach positioned the program management life cycle as the predominant thread throughout the entire standard document. In addition, a structure for the standard was adopted that mirrored the layout and format of PMI's project management standard, the *PMBOK® Guide*. Within this structure, the program standard described specific program management Process Groups and Knowledge Areas. With this framework in place, the Second Edition revealed a clearly evident life-cycle-based, "process orientation" to the presentation of program management work and the role of the program manager.

- ◆ **Third Edition.** Considering the previous two editions, emphasis for the Third edition was on usefulness and readability. Careful analysis of the most effective elements of the earlier editions resulted in a decision to change from the Second edition's structure that paralleled the *PMBOK® Guide*'s Process Groups, Knowledge Areas, and inputs/tools and techniques/outputs in favor of the domain-oriented presentation of the First Edition.

Within the Third Edition, the following key changes were made:

- The return to the domain-orientation of the First Edition,
- The focus on the program management performance domains presented in the role delineation study (RDS),
- The benefits of the learnings and advancements derived from both previous editions of PMI's *The Standard for Program Management,* and
- An alignment to, and recognition of, other standards and writings in program management from outside the United States.

◆ **Fourth Edition.** It was determined that significant changes between the Third and Fourth Editions were not necessary, and changes instead focused on addressing deferred comments from the Third Edition update as well as comments submitted by subject matter experts through an internal review and exposure draft process. Given that a major update occurred between the Second and Third Editions through the shift to a principle-based approach, it was also an opportunity to increase consistency throughout the eight sections. Table X1-1 summarizes major changes across the sections:

Table X1-1. Fourth Edition High Level Changes

Change Applied	Description
Expanded Section 1 to address key program roles	Absorbed key content from the Appendix X3: *categorization of programs, program manager competencies* Expanded the introduction to critical roles: *program manager, program sponsor, and program management office*
Section 2 was refined to address program complexity and interdependency	Added a subsection on program complexity and interdependency Shifted introduction of program life cycle phases into Section 7
Section 3 was expanded	Expanded to address program risk strategy
Section 5 was expanded	Expanded to address program stakeholder mapping and program stakeholder communication
Aligned Section 6 on Program Governance to the PMI's new Practice Guide on Governance	PMI published a new Practice Guide -- *Governance of Portfolios, Programs, and Projects: A Practice Guide.* A careful review of the sections addressing program governance was performed so that both publications align. The standard and practice guide now reflect consistency in description of roles. Expanded to address the roles associated within program governance Content reorganized with activity-based content shifted to Section 8
Section 7 broadened to introduce life cycle phases	Absorbed introduction to life cycle phases Relabeled "program benefits delivery phase" to "program delivery phase" Added an introduction to program activities to segue into Section 8
Refreshed Section 8	As the standard continues to shift closer to being principle-based, versus process-based, Section 8 shifted away from supporting "processes" to supporting "program activities." A major change to the structure of Section 8 also occurred to assist practitioners in mapping Sections 3 through 7 with the content of Section 8. Program activities are now aligned to the program life cycle phases versus topics.
Focused on harmonization and alignment across the sections in the standard, and removed duplicate or redundant artifacts	Program artifacts that were not explained or utilized were removed. Careful detail was also placed on harmonizing the descriptions of artifacts across the various sections.
Updated the definitions of *program* and *program management*	**Program.** Related projects, subsidiary programs, and program activities managed in a coordinated manner to obtain benefits not available from managing them individually. **Program Management.** The application of knowledge, skills, and principles to a program to achieve the program objectives and to obtain benefits and control not available by managing program components individually.

X1.3.2 PROGRAM MANAGEMENT CONTENT

The Standard for Program Management – Fourth Edition presents concepts and practices unique to program management and does not imitate, copy, or represent concepts or processes that are easily referenced in the vast body of project management literature. Where program management processes rely on or may be performed similarly to those found in the project management domain, the user is directed to documentation and relevant readings in project management.

X1.4 OVERVIEW OF SECTIONS

Sections X1.4.1 through X1.4.8 describe each section of the standard and detail the changes the reader will find when comparing the Second and Third Editions.

X1.4.1 SECTION 1—INTRODUCTION

Minor changes were made throughout Section 1 to improve consistency within the standard and to ensure that key concepts covered in Sections 2 through 8 were introduced early in the document.

In Section 1.2 the role of programs in delivering benefits via the outcomes and outputs of component activities was emphasized. The term subsidiary program, which was defined as a program sponsored by another program, was also introduced.

In Section 1.3, the importance of ensuring that program components remain strategically aligned with the organization's goals was emphasized.

Section 1.4 addressed the differences and interactions between program management and project management in greater detail, emphasizing the iterative nature of programs.

Content from the Third Edition appendix was absorbed into Section 1 in order to expand the discussion of roles important to programs, including the role of the program sponsor and the program management office. Section 1.7.1 was also expanded to enhance the descriptions of important program manager skills including: communication, stakeholder engagement, change management, leadership, analysis, and component integration skills.

As with the previous editions, effort was made to harmonize this section with other PMI foundational standards. Table X1-2 outlines the revised Section 1.

Table X1-2. Section 1 – Fourth Edition

Section 1	Introduction
1.1	**Purpose of *The Standard for Program Management***
1.2	**What is a Program?**
1.2.1	Initiation of Programs
1.2.2	The Relationships Among Portfolios, Programs, and Projects
1.3	**What is Program Management?**
1.4	**The Relationships Among Portfolio, Program, and Project Management, and their Roles in Organizational Project Management (OPM)**
1.4.1	The Interactions Among Portfolio, Program, and Project Management
1.4.2	The Relationship Between Program Management and Portfolio Management
1.4.3	The Relationship Between Program Management and Project Management
1.5	**The Relationships Among Organizational Strategy, Program Management, and Operations Management**
1.6	**Business Value**
1.7	**Role of the Program Manager**
1.7.1	Program Manager Competences
1.8	**Role of the Program Sponsor**
1.9	**Role of the Program Management Office**

X1.4.2 SECTION 2—PROGRAM MANAGEMENT PERFORMANCE DOMAINS

Section 2 maintained the focus on explaining the Program Management Performance Domains and discussing and documenting the characteristics that uniquely define program management as something different from project management and portfolio management.

Sections 2.1.1 (Program Life Cycle Phases) was removed from Section 2. The rationale is that the focus of Section 2 is on the explanation of the Program Management Performance Domains. The Program Life Cycle is discussed in detail in Section 7. In addition, Section 2.1.2 was also removed and moved to Section 7.

The logical flow of this section was addressed with Section 2.5 (Third Edition) moving to Section 2.3 (Fourth Edition). This provides this section with a more top-down approach. The differences between a portfolio, a program, and a project were revised. The logical order was changed to first discuss the difference between a portfolio and a program and then the difference between a program and a project. Three distinctions are made between a program and a project in this edition (complexity, change, and uncertainty) versus the two distinctions in the Third Edition (change and uncertainty).

Refer to Table X1-3 for an overview of the Section 2.

Table X1-3. Section 2 – Fourth Edition

Section 2	Program Management Performance Domains
2.1	**Program Management Performance Domain Definitions**
2.2	**Program Management Performance Domain Interactions**
2.3	**Organizational Strategy, Portfolio Management, and Program Management Linkage**
2.4	**Portfolio and Program Distinctions**
2.5	**Program and Project Distinctions**
2.5.1	Uncertainty
2.5.2	Managing Change
2.5.3	Complexity

X1.4.3 SECTION 3—PROGRAM STRATEGY ALIGNMENT

To further enhance the Program Strategy Alignment Performance Domain, the Fourth Edition added Program Risk Management Strategy as a means for ensuring the program is aligned with organizational strategy. The program risk management strategy is developed by defining program risk thresholds, performing the initial program risk assessment, and developing a high-level program risk response strategy, which will then be used to guide program risk management activities (actively identifying, monitoring, analyzing, accepting, mitigating, avoiding, or retiring program risk).

Other changes in Section 3 were minor and mainly included moving process level details to Section 8 while retaining high-level descriptions in this section.

Table X1-4 shows the content of Section 3 in the Fourth Edition.

Table X1-4. Section 3 – Fourth Edition

Section 3	Program Strategy Alignment
3.1	**Program Business Case**
3.2	**Program Charter**
3.3	**Program Roadmap**
3.4	**Environmental Assessments**
3.4.1	Enterprise Environmental Factors
3.4.2	Environmental Analysis
3.5	**Program Risk Management Strategy**
3.5.1	Risk Management for Strategy Alignment
3.5.2	Program Risk Thresholds
3.5.3	Initial Program Risk Assessment
3.5.4	Program Risk Response Strategy

X1.4.4 SECTION 4—PROGRAM BENEFITS MANAGEMENT

Section 4 was updated to address risk management with regard to benefits management. This included risk mitigation and risk. This section was refined to be in agreement with the updates to the life cycle. Nomenclature was updated to agree with newly adopted terminology within the standard.

Figures and tables were updated to agree with the new text and the remainder of the standard.

Table X1-5 provides an overview of Section 4.

Table X1-5. Section 4 Fourth Edition

Section 4	Program Benefits Management
4.1	**Benefits Identification**
4.1.1	Benefits Register
4.2	**Benefits Analysis and Planning**
4.2.1	Benefits Management Plan
4.2.2	Benefits Management and the Program Roadmap
4.2.3	Benefits Register Update
4.3	**Benefits Delivery**
4.3.1	Benefits and Program Components
4.3.2	Benefits and Program Governance
4.4	**Benefits Transition**
4.5	**Benefits Sustainment**

X1.4.5 SECTION 5—PROGRAM STAKEHOLDER ENGAGEMENT

Program Stakeholder Engagement appeared in the First Edition of the standard as one of the three themes in program management, along with benefits realization and governance. This domain is focused on stakeholder engagement rather than stakeholder management because the work of the program manager in organizations is to ensure the direct and frequent engagement of stakeholders and the active management of each engagement. In the Fourth Edition, the information was expanded by elaborating on stakeholder analysis and communication. These aspects are critical to understanding the organizational culture, politics, and concerns related to the program, as well as the overall impact, which in turn may impact or influence the delivery of benefits by the program.

Table X1-6 provides an overview of Section 5.

Table X1-6. Section 5 – Fourth Edition

Section 5	Program Stakeholder Engagement
5.1	Program Stakeholder Identification
5.2	Program Stakeholder Analysis
5.3	Program Stakeholder Engagement Planning
5.4	Program Stakeholder Engagement
5.5	Program Stakeholder Communication

X1.4.6 PROGRAM GOVERNANCE

Program governance appeared in the First Edition of the standard as one of the three themes in program management, along with benefits realization and stakeholder management. In the Fourth Edition, program governance is detailed as one of the four Program Management Performance Domains which enables and performs program decision making, establishes practices to support the program, and maintains program oversight. The focus is on the program governance practices and the governance roles required to perform them.

Where appropriate, the Fourth Edition leverages and aligns with Section 4 of *Governance of Portfolios, Programs, and Projects: A Practice Guide* covering roles and responsibilities and program and governance relationships. Specific synergies between sections covering 'Roles and Responsibilities' and 'Program and Governance Relationships' are included.

This edition introduces a description of the environment and organizational factors and the program attributes which the design of program governance accommodates (see Table X1-7). Content was also reorganized with activity-based content shifting to Section 8, where appropriate.

Table X1-7. Section 6 – Fourth Edition

Section 6	Program Governance
6.1	**Program Governance Practices**
6.1.1	Program Governance Plan
6.1.2	Program Governance and Vision and Goals
6.1.3	Program Approval, Endorsement, and Definition
6.1.4	Program Success Criteria
6.2.5	Program Monitoring, Reporting, and Controlling
6.1.6	Program Risk and Issue Governance
6.1.7	Program Quality Governance
6.1.8	Program Change Governance
6.1.9	Program Governance Reviews
6.1.10	Program Periodic Health Checks
6.1.11	Program Component Initiation and Transition
6.1.12	Program Closure
6.2	**Program Governance Roles**
6.2.1	Program Sponsor
6.2.2	Program Steering Committee
6.2.3	The Program Management Office
6.2.4	Program Manager
6.2.5	Project Manager(s)
6.2.6	Other Stakeholders
6.3	**Program Governance Design and Implementation**

X1.4.7 PROGRAM

The Fourth Edition expands the program life cycle management section to emphasize the importance of program integration management. This is a core activity that occurs across the program life cycle. As a result, activities related to program integration management that were associated with the program level supporting activities have been relocated from Section 8 to Section 7. This update serves to provide a more complete explanation of how integration management combines, unifies, and coordinates the work of multiple components within the program.

Additionally, the Program Benefits Delivery phase has been renamed to Program Delivery. This change seeks to draw a clear distinction between the major phases of the program life cycle and the activities that are performed as part of Benefits Delivery in the Benefits Management performance domain. The Program Delivery phase includes the benefits analysis and planning activities, in addition to, the benefits delivery activities. It encompasses all the work required to deliver the intended benefits, such as prioritizing, initiating, planning, and executing the program components, as well as, monitoring each component to ensure its benefits are aligned to the benefit realization plan.

These key elements represent the evolution of program life cycle management and how program activities that are performed to support the individual components in achieving the overall program objectives.

Table X1-8 provides an overview of Section 7.

Table X1-8. Section 7 – Fourth Edition

Section 7	Program Life Cycle Management
7.1	**The Program Life Cycle**
7.1.1	Program Life Cycle Phases Overview
7.1.2	Program Definition Phase
7.1.3	Program Delivery Phase
7.1.4	Program Closure Phase
7.2	**Program Activities and Integration Management**
7.2.1	Program Activities Overview
7.2.2	Program Integration Management
7.2.3	Mapping of the Program Life Cycle to Program Activities

X1.4.8 PROGRAM ACTIVITIES

In the Third Edition, Section 8 was structured along the lines of program management supporting processes, including Program Financial Management, Scope Management, Communications Management, Procurement Management, and others, which provide the needed process information to complement Program Life Cycle Management, as described in Section 7. The Fourth Edition committee considered it more effective to align Section 8 with Section 7 by restructuring the material into program life cycle phases and describing the activities that support each phase. Program Change Management was introduced as a Program Activity to enable more formal planning, monitoring, and controlling of change during Program Definition and Delivery. Finally, Program Information Management was described as a Program Activity separate from Program Communications Management, recognizing the importance of managing program information resources and reflecting current best practices.

Table X1-9 provides an overview of Section 8.

Table X1-9. Section 8 - Fourth Edition

Section 8	Program Activities
8.1	**Program Definition Phase Activities**
8.1.1	Program Formulation Activities
8.1.2	Program Planning Activities
8.2	**Program Delivery Phase Activities**
8.2.1	Program Change Monitoring and Controlling
8.2.2	Program Communications Management
8.2.3	Program Financial Management
8.2.4	Program Information Management
8.2.5	Program Procurement Management
8.2.6	Program Quality Assurance and Control
8.2.7	Program Resource Management
8.2.8	Program Risk Monitoring and Controlling
8.2.9	Program Schedule Monitoring and Controlling
8.2.10	Program Scope Monitoring and Controlling
8.3	**Program Closure Phase Activities**
8.3.1	Program Financial Closure
8.3.2	Program Information Archiving and Transition
8.3.3	Program Procurement Closure
8.3.4	Program Resource Transition
8.3.5	Program Risk Management Transition

APPENDIX X2
CONTRIBUTORS AND REVIEWERS FOR *THE STANDARD FOR PROGRAM MANAGEMENT*—FOURTH EDITION

This appendix lists, within groupings, those individuals who have contributed to the development and production of *The Standard for Program Management*–Fourth Edition.

The Project Management Institute is grateful to all of these individuals for their support and acknowledges their contributions to the project management profession.

X2.1 *THE STANDARD FOR PROGRAM MANAGEMENT* —FOURTH EDITION CORE COMMITTEE

The following individuals served as members, were contributors of text or concepts, and served as leaders within the Project Core Committee:

Vanina Mangano, PMP, PMI-RMP, Chair
Carolina Gabriela Spindola, PMP, CSSBB, Vice Chair
Brad Bigelow, PMP, MSP
Shika Carter, PgMP, PMP
Colette J. Connor, PMP
Wanda Curlee PfMP, PgMP
Richard J. Heaslip, PhD
Felicia Elizabeth Hong, MBA, PMP
Carl Marnewick, PhD
Anca Slușanschi, PMP, MSc
Maricarmen Suarez, PMP, PgMP
Kristin L. Vitello
Andy Wright, MBA, BSc (Hons)

X2.2 *THE STANDARD FOR PROGRAM MANAGEMENT* —FOURTH EDITION CONTENT COMMITTEE

The following individuals were contributors of text or concepts and provided recommendations on drafts of *The Standard for Program Management*–Fourth Edition:

Chris Richards, PMP
Terry Lee Ricci, PfMP, PgMP
Daniele Pinto, PMP

X2.3 REVIEWERS

X2.3.1 SME REVIEW

In addition to the members of the Committee, the following individuals provided their review and recommendations on drafts of the standard:

Emad E. Aziz, PfMP, PgMP
Martial Bellec, PgMP, PMI-ACP
James F. Carilli, PfMP, PgMP
David M. Ciriello, PgMP, PMP
Sandy Hoath Cobb, PfMP, PgMP
Christopher L. Edwards MBA, PMP
Scott Girard
Jean Gouix, Eng, PgMP PMP
Ginger Levin, PhD, PgMP, PMP

Jamie Mines
Marvin R. Nelson, MBA, SCPM
Eric S. Norman, PgMP, PMI Fellow
Crispin ("Kik") Piney, BSc, PfMP
Sandra E. Smalley
Matthew D. Tomlinson, PgMP, PMP
Michel Thiry, PhD, PMI Fellow
Gwen Whitman, EMBA, PfMP

X2.3.2 FINAL EXPOSURE DRAFT REVIEWERS

In addition to the members of the Committee, the following individuals provided recommendations for improving the Exposure Draft of the *The Standard for Program Management*–Fourth Edition:

Galal Abdelmessih, FEC, PMP
Habeeb Abdulla, PMP, RMP
Ali Abedi, PhD, PMP
Tarik Al Hraki, PMP, P3O
Homam Al Khateeb, PMP, ACP
Abubaker Sami Ali, PfMP, PgMP
Bill Allbee, PMP
Wasel Al-Muhammad
Charalampos Apostolopoulos,
    PhD, PMP
Vijaya Chandar Avula
Nabeel Eltyeb Babiker, PMP, P3O
Manikandan Bangarusamy,
    PgMP,PMP
Manuel F. Baquero V., MSc, PMP
Thomas Charles Belanger,
    MS, PMP
Shantanu Bhamare, PMP, LIMC
Nigel Blampied, PE, PMP
Greta Blash, PMP, PMI-ACP
Raúl Borges, PMP
Farid F. Bouges, PhD, PfMP, PMP
Alberto S. Brito, MSc
James F. Carilli, PfMP, PgMP
Christopher W. Carson, PMP, CCM
Sergio Luis Conte, PhD
Jesús Cruz-Franco, PgMP, PMP
Larry C. Dalton, PgMP
Shauna Daly
Farshid Damirchilo, MSc, PMP
Jean-Michel De Jaeger Emba, PMP
Kaushal Desai
Saju Devassy, PMP, ITIL
Ivana Dilparic
Yasir Elsadig, PfMP, PMP
Majdi N. Elyyan, PMP, PMI-RMP
Diego H. Escobar, PMP
Sergio Ferreto Gutiérrez,
    MPM, MBA

Nestor C. Gabarda Jr., PMP, MSP
Ravindra Gajendragadkar,
    PMP, MSP
Robert M. Galbraith, PMP
Theofanis Giotis, PMP, PMI-ACP
Jean Gouix
Scott M. Graffius, PMP
Simon Harris, CGEIT, PRINCE2Agile
Patti Harter, PMP
Henry Hattenrath
Susumu Hayakawa, PMP
Hironori Hayashi, PMP, PMI-PBA
Bruce A. Hayes PMP, CSM
Gheorghe Hriscu, PMP, CGEIT
Mamane Ibrahim, PMP, CMQOE
Shuichi Ikeda
Masako Imamura, PMP
Suhail Iqbal, PfMP, PgMP
Frank E. Jakob, PE, PMP
Anand Jayaraman, PMP
Hernan Dario Jimenez
Robert Joslin, PhD, PfMP
Shoichiro Kashimura
Suhail Khaled
Ahmed S. Khalil, Eng, OPM3, PMP
Adeel Khan
Henry Kondo, PfMP, PMP
Ryohei Kondo, PMP
Maciej Koszykowski,
    PMP, PMI-RMP
Mahesh Kuimil, PE, PgMP
Avinash Kumar, PMP
Cristian Lagos
Harisha Lakkavalli, PMP, PgMP
G. Lakshmi Sekhar, PMP, PMI-SP
Craig Letavec, PfMP
Lydia G. Liberio, JD, PMP
Tong Liu, PhD, PMP
Zheng Lou, PgMP, MBA

Lucas Machuca
Sanjay Mandhan
Gaitan Marius Titi, PMP
Lou Marks, PMP
Constance Martin-Wilson
Gary Marx, MBA, PMP
Puian Masudi Far, PhDc, PMP
Sandeep Mathur, PgMP, FAICD
Thomas F. McCabe, CSSMBB, PMP
Mohammed M'hamdi, PMP
Lubomira Mihailova, MBA, PMP
Akiyoshi Miki, PMP
Gloria Miller
Venkatramvasi Mohanvasi, PMP
Mordaka Maciej, PMP
Syed Ahsan Mustaqeem, PE, PMP
Faig Nasibov, PMP
Marvin R. Nelson, MBA, SCPM
Jeffrey S. Nielsen, PgMP, PMP
Eric S. Norman, PgMP, PMI Fellow
Allan Old, PGDipPM, PMP
Habeeb Omar, PfMP, PgMP
Stefan Ondek, PMP
Hariyo Pangarso
Seenivasan Pavanasam,
    PgMP, PfMP
Jean-Pierre Pericaud
Crispin ("Kik") Piney, BSc, PfMP
Svetlana Prahova, PMP
S. Ramani, PgMP, PfMP
Christopher S. Rambo, PgMP, PMP
P. Ravikumar, PMP, PMI-ACP
Michael Reed, PfMP, PMP
Alexander V. Revin, PMP
Juan Carlos Ribero
Bernard Roduit
Stelian Roman, PMP, PMI-ACP
P. Fernando Romero, MBA, PMP

Rafael Fernando Ronces Rosas, PMP, ITIL

Parthasarathy Sampath

Edward Shehab, PfMP, PgMP,

Toshiki Shimoike, PhD, PMP

Sandeep Shouche, PgMP, PMI-ACP

Gary J. Sikma, PMP, PMI-ACP

Mauro Sotille, PMP, PMI-RMP

Howard Souder, Jr., CPCM, CFCM

Pranay Srivastava, PMP, CSM

Shoji Tajima, MS, PMP

Tetsuya Tani, PMP

Sivasubramanian Thangarathnam, BE, PMP

Matthew D. Tomlinson, PgMP, PMP

Ali Vahedi Diz, PfMP, PgMP

Raymond Z. van Tonder B-Tech, PMP

Toshiyuki Henry Watanabe, PE, JP, PMP

Lars Wendestam, MSc, PMP

Deb Whitcomb, MBA, PMP

Michal P. Wieteska, PMP

Karen Wright

Yan Wu, PMP, SPC4

Clement C. L. Yeung, PMP

Kenichi Yoshida, PMP, ITC

Marcin Żmigrodzki, PhD, PgMP

X2.4 PMI STANDARDS PROGRAM MEMBER ADVISORY GROUP (MAG)

The following individuals served as members of the PMI Standards Program Member Advisory Group during development of the *The Standard for Program Management*–Fourth Edition:

Maria Cristina Barbero, PMI-ACP, PMP

Brian Grafsgaard, PgMP, PMP

Hagit Landman, PMP, PMI-SP

Yvan Petit PhD, PMP

Chris Stevens, PhD

Dave Violette, MPM, PMP

John Zlockie, MBA, PMP, PMI Standards Manager

X2.5 CONSENSUS BODY REVIEW

The following individuals served as members of the PMI Standards Program Consensus Body:

Chris Cartwright, MPM

John L. Dettbarn, Jr., DSc, PE

Charles T. Follin, PMP

Dana J. Goulston, PMP

Brian Grafsgaard, PgMP, PMP

Dave Gunner, MSc, PMP

Dorothy L. Kangas, PMP

Thomas M. Kurihara

Hagit Landman, PMP, PMI-SP

Timothy A. MacFadyen, MBA, MPM

Harold "Mike" Mosley, Jr., PE, PMP

Eric S. Norman, PgMP, PMI Fellow

Nanette Patton, MSBA, PMP

Yvan Petit, PhD, PMP

Michael Reed, PfMP, PM

David W. Ross, PgMP, PMP

Paul E. Shaltry, PMP

Chris Stevens, PhD

Geree V. Streun, PMP, PMI-ACP

Dave Violette, MPM, PMP

X2.6 PRODUCTION STAFF

Special mention is due to the following employees of PMI:

Donn Greenberg, Manager, Publications

Roberta Storer, Product Editor

Barbara Walsh, Publications Production Supervisor

GLOSSARY

1. INCLUSIONS AND EXCLUSIONS

This glossary includes terms that are:

◆ Unique to program management (e.g., benefits management).

◆ Not unique to program management, but used differently or with a narrower meaning in program management than in general everyday usage (e.g., benefit, risk).

This glossary generally does not include:

◆ Application or industry area-specific terms.

◆ Terms used in program management which do not differ in any material way from everyday use (e.g., business outcome).

◆ Terms used in program management which do not differ from a similar term defined in the *PMBOK® Guide* – Sixth Edition, except that these terms are now used at a program level instead of a project level (e.g. a program charter and a project charter both serve the same purpose—to approve the start of the effort).

Many of the words defined in this glossary may have broader and, in some cases, different dictionary definitions to accommodate the context of program management.

2. DEFINITIONS

Benefit. The gains and assets realized by the organization and other stakeholders as the result of outcomes delivered by the program.

Benefits Management Plan. The documented explanation defining the processes for creating, maximizing, and sustaining the benefits provided by a project or program.

Benefits Analysis and Planning Phase. Establishes the program benefits management plan and develops the benefits metrics and framework for monitoring and controlling both the components and the measurement of benefits within the program.

Benefits Delivery Phase. Ensures that the program delivers the expected benefits, as defined in the benefits management plan.

Benefits Identification Phase. Analyzes the available information about organizational and business strategies, internal and external influences, and program drivers to identify and qualify the benefits that program stakeholders expect to realize.

Benefits Sustainment Phase. Ongoing maintenance activities performed beyond the end of the program by receiving organizations to assure continued generation of the improvements and outcomes delivered by the program.

Benefits Transition Phase. Program activities that ensure that benefits are transitioned to operational areas and can be sustained once they are transferred.

Business Case. A documented economic feasibility study used to establish validity of the benefits to be delivered by a program.

Component. A project, subsidiary program, or other related activity conducted to support a program.

Constraint. A factor that limits the options for managing a project, program, portfolio, or process.

Enterprise Environmental Factors. Conditions not under the immediate control of the team that influence, constrain, or direct the project, program, or portfolio.

Performing Organization. An enterprise whose personnel are the most directly involved in doing the work of the project or program.

Phase Gate. A review at the end of a phase in which a decision is made to continue to the next phase, to continue with modification, or to end a project or program.

Portfolio. Projects, programs, subsidiary portfolios, and operations managed as a group to achieve strategic objectives.

Portfolio Management. The centralized management of one or more portfolios to achieve strategic objectives.

Procurement Management Plan. A component of the project or program management plan that describes how a team will acquire goods and services from outside of the performing organization.

Program. Related projects, subsidiary programs, and program activities managed in a coordinated manner to obtain benefits not available from managing them individually.

Program Activities. Tasks and work conducted to support a program and which contribute throughout the program life cycle.

Program Benefits Management. Processes that clarify the program's planned benefits and intended outcomes and processes for monitoring the program's ability to deliver against these benefits and outcomes.

Program Benefits Management Performance Domain. Performance domain that defines, creates, maximizes, and delivers the benefits provided by the program.

Program Change Management. Activities to plan for, monitor, control, and administer changes during the course of the program.

Program Charter. A document issued by a sponsor that authorizes the program management team to use organizational resources to execute the program and links the program to the organization's strategic objectives.

Program Closure Phase. Program activities necessary to transition program benefits to sustaining organization and formally close the program in a controlled manner.

Program Communications Management. Activities necessary for the timely and appropriate generation, collection, distribution, storage, retrieval, and ultimate disposition of program information.

Program Definition Phase. Program activities conducted to authorize the program and develop the program roadmap required to achieve the expected results.

Program Delivery Phase. Program activities performed to produce the intended results of each component in accordance with the program management plan.

Program Financial Framework. A high-level initial plan for coordinating available funding, determining constraints, and determining how funding is allocated.

Program Financial Management. Activities related to identifying the program's financial sources and resources, integrating the budgets of the program components, developing the overall budget for the program, and controlling costs during the program.

Program Governance. The framework, functions, and processes by which a program is monitored, managed, and supported in order to meet organizational strategic and operational goals.

Program Governance Framework. The supporting structure around which the decision making, supporting, and oversight practices are constructed, operated, and managed.

Program Governance Performance Domain. Performance domain that enables and performs program decision making, establishes practices to support the program, and maintains program oversight.

Program Governance Plan. A document that describes the systems and methods to be used to monitor, manage, and support a given program, and the responsibilities of specific roles for ensuring the timely and effective use of those systems and methods.

Program Information Management. Activities related to how the program's information assets are prepared, collected, organized, and secured.

Program Information Management Plan. A component of the program management plan that describes how the program's information assets will be prepared, collected, and organized.

Program Integration Management. Program activities conducted to identify, define, combine, unify, and coordinate multiple components within the program.

Program Life Cycle Management. Managing all program activities related to program definition, program delivery, and program closure.

Program Life Cycle Management Performance Domain. Performance domain that manages program activities required to facilitate effective program definition, program delivery, and program closure.

Program Management. The application of knowledge, skills, and principles to a program to achieve the program objectives and to obtain benefits and control not available by managing program components individually.

Program Management Information Systems. Tools used to collect, integrate, and communicate information critical for the effective management of one or more organizational programs.

Program Management Office. A management structure that standardizes the program-related governance processes and facilitates the sharing of resources, methodologies, tools, and techniques.

Program Management Performance Domain. Complementary groupings of related areas of activity or function that uniquely characterize and differentiate the activities found in one performance domain from the others within the full scope of program management work.

Program Management Plan. A document that integrates the program's subsidiary plans and establishes the management controls and overall plan for integrating and managing the program's individual components.

Program Manager. The person authorized by the performing organization to lead the team or teams responsible for achieving program objectives.

Program Master Schedule. An output of a schedule model that logically links components, milestones, and high-level activities necessary to deliver program benefits.

Program Procurement Management. The application of knowledge, skills, tools, and techniques necessary to acquire products and services to meet the needs of the overall program and the constituent projects/components.

Program Quality Assurance. The activities related to the periodic evaluation of overall program quality to provide confidence that the program will comply with relevant quality policies and standards.

Program Quality Control. The monitoring of specific components or program deliverables and results to determine if they meet the quality requirements and lead to benefits realization.

Program Quality Management. The activities of the performing organization that determine program quality policies, objectives, and responsibilities so that the program will be successful.

Program Resource Management. Program activities that ensure all required resources (people, equipment, material, etc.) are made available to the component managers to enable the delivery of benefits for the program.

Program Schedule Management. An activity to determine the order and timing of the components needed to produce the program benefits, estimate the amount of time required to accomplish each one, identify significant milestones during the performance of the program, and document the outcomes of each milestone.

Program Risk. An uncertain event or condition that, if it occurs, has a positive or negative effect on the program.

Program Risk Management. Program activities related to actively identifying, monitoring, analyzing, accepting, mitigating, avoiding, or retiring program risk.

Program Risk Register. A document in which risks are recorded together with the results of risk analysis and risk response planning.

Program Roadmap. A chronological representation of a program's intended direction that graphically depicts dependencies between major milestones and decision points and reflects the linkage between the business strategy and the program work.

Program Scope Management. Activities that define, develop, monitor, control, and verify program scope.

Program Stakeholder Engagement Performance Domain. Performance domain that identifies and analyzes stakeholder needs and manages expectations and communications to foster stakeholder support.

Program Strategy Alignment. Activities associated with the integration and development of business strategies and organizational goals and objectives, and the degree to which operations and performance meet stated organizational goals and objectives.

Program Strategy Alignment Performance Domain. Performance domain that identifies program outputs and outcomes to provide benefits aligned with the organization's goals and objectives.

Program Steering Committee. Group of participants representing various program-related interests with the purpose of supporting the program under its authority by providing guidance, endorsements, and approvals through the governance practices. This committee may also be referred to as Program Governance Board.

Project. A temporary endeavor undertaken to create a unique product, service, or result.

Project Management. The application of knowledge, skills, tools, and techniques to project activities to meet the project requirements.

Quality Management Plan. A component of the project or program management plan that describes how an organization's policies, procedures, and guidelines will be implemented to achieve the quality objectives.

Risk Management Plan. A component of the project, program, or portfolio management plan that describes how risk management activities will be structured and performed.

Schedule Management Plan. A component of the project or program management plan that establishes the criteria for developing, monitoring, and controlling the schedule.

Scope Management Plan. A component of the project or program management plan that describes how the scope will be defined, developed, monitored, controlled, and validated.

Sponsor. An individual or a group that provides resources and support for the project, program, or portfolio, and is accountable for enabling success.

Stakeholder. An individual, group, or organization that may affect, be affected by, or perceive itself to be affected by a decision, activity, or outcome of a project, program, or portfolio.

INDEX

E

Economic feasibility study. *See* Business case
Endorsement, program, 72
Enterprise environmental factors
    definition, 164
    environmental assessments and, 38–39
Environmental analysis, 39–40
Environmental assessments, 38–40
    enterprise environmental factors, 38–39
    environmental analysis, 39–40
Ethics, 2
Expectation management, 58

F

Failure, risk of, 86
Feasibility studies, 40
Financial management. *See also* Program financial
    management
    funding models and, 114
    program financial closure, 138
Financial management plan, 116
Funding organization
    financial framework and, 114
    as key program stakeholder, 61
Funding structure, program, 87

G

Generally recognized, definition, 2
Goals
    program governance and, 71
    strategic plan and, 35
Good practice, definition, 2
Governance. *See also* Program governance
    activities supporting, 105
    complexity, 31
    hierarchy, 68
    plan, 70
    portfolio, 68
    risk monitoring and, 54
Guide to the Project Management Body of Knowledge
(*PMBOK® Guide*), A. *See PMBOK® Guide*

H

Health checks, program, 76
Hierarchy
    decision-making, 86
    program governance, 68
Historical information analysis, 40

I

IFB (invitation for bid), 131
Impact analysis, 65
Implementing Organizational Project Management:
    A Practice Guide, 1, 10
Information. *See also* Program information management
    exchange of, 14
    program information archiving and transition, 139–140
    program information distribution methods, 126
Information management plan, 116
Initiation of programs, 6–7
Integration skills, 18
Interdependencies. *See also* Dependencies
    complexity of, 31
    coordination of, 13
    program components and, 9, 121, 122
    resource interdependency planning, 133
Invitation for bid (IFB), 131
Issue(s)
    escalation processes, 73
    management of, 13
    stakeholder, 65
Issue log, 65

K

Key performance indicators
    benefits register and, 47
    governance and, 52
Knowledge management, 102. *See also* Lessons learned

L

Leadership skills, 18
Legislative environment, 86
Lessons learned, 102
    database, 130
Life cycle. *See* Program life cycle; Program Life Cycle
    Management Performance Domain